"Corey throws out a life preserver to anyone caught in the swirling waters of grief. All one has to do is grab a hold and she will gentle draw you back to safety and wellness again."

–Sherry Zak Morris, CEO, Yoga Journey Productions

"What a brilliant work illuminating the path of the griever, but also illuminating new possibilities. Corey invites us to go with her on an amazing journey to the awareness that while grief is a timeless aspect of our life experience, it can lead us to open doors to a joyful life that we would not imagine possible after a significant loss."

–Kevin Kaiser, Co-founder, Kaiser Institute

A fantastic book! Powerful, practical, and solid advice on tackling the really hard aspects of grief in a very loving transformative way! I came away from this book feeling so inspired and with a much greater context for the often narrow field of grief.

-Sarah Entrup, Founder of Free the She

"*Grief Interrupted*" is a book that reaches out and touches your heart. In sharing the story of how she lost her daughter, Corey Stiles reminds us that living with grief is not only possible, but that more importantly, it has a significant role to play in our healing. She walks us through the steps she used herself to recover from the emotional impact of her loss; steps that we often avoid, incorrectly assuming they will add to our pain. Instead, Corey shows us how each step is essential to the resolution of the trauma and how we can grow in spite of grief. Beautifully laid out, these steps make up a path we can use again and again as we deal with the sometimes unexpected and painful circumstances of life."

–Sandi Amorim, Master Coach and author of
The 100 Day Promise

"What a healing, supportive, gentle reminder that grief is a journey that we all experience, and also that, rather than getting mired in the depths of grief, we can also reclaim joy as part of the path. *Grief Interrupted* highlights a road map of tools including allowing nature to soften you, relieving tension in the body, and cultivating more pleasure. Corey Stiles has written a lovely and supportive guide!"

–Sue Rasmussen, Clutter Coach and best-selling author of
My Desk Is Driving Me Crazy

"What a heart-centered, gentle book to guide you through the process of grief, and open you up to reclaim life and joy. *Grief Interrupted* is written by someone who knows what they're talking about, including the effects of grief on not only your mindset and emotional state, but on your body - and shares simple, obvious steps that aren't so simple or obvious when you are in the midst of a devastatingly dark storm of emotion. *Grief Interrupted* would be the book to pick up when you've had some time to process the shock of loss and are even vaguely thinking about toeing past the line of all-consuming grief and want to see if you can be happy again."

–Sara Blanchard, mother's happiness advocate and
best-selling author of *Flex Mom*

Grief Interrupted

Grief Interrupted

A Holistic Guide to Reclaiming Your Joy

Published in New York, New York, by Morgan James Publishing. Morgan James is a trademark of Morgan James, LLC. www.MorganJamesPublishing.com

The Morgan James Speakers Group can bring authors to your live event. For more information or to book an event visit The Morgan James Speakers Group at www.TheMorganJamesSpeakersGroup.com.

ISBN 9781683505518   PB
ISBN 9781683505525   EB
Library of Congress
Control Number: 2017906033

Front Cover Designer: Glen Edelstein

Interior Design by: Glen Edelstein

In an effort to support local communities, raise awareness and funds, Morgan James Publishing donates a percentage of all book sales for the life of each book to Habitat for Humanity Peninsula and Greater Williamsburg.

Get involved today! Visit
www.MorganJamesBuilds.com

Grief
Interrupted

A Holistic Guide to
Reclaiming Your Joy

COREY STILES

NEW YORK

LONDON • NASHVILLE • MELBOURNE • VANCOUVER

For Aleisha:

Master Lightbringer

Contents

Foreword

ARE YOU THE KIND OF PERSON who talks to perfect strangers on planes?

If you're flying by yourself–whether for business or "whilst on holiday"–are you likely to strike up a conversation with someone you've never met?

I've always kinda admired those people who are good at that–carrying on with some person they just randomly met seconds ago–chatting it up in that spirited, small-talk way that some people do. My Mom is the all-time best. She'll jibber-jabber with just about anyone at any time.

But I am NOT one of those people.

For me, flying–when solo– is a "sanctuary" experience. And I fly a lot. 1.57 million miles lifetime.

In all those miles, and on all those flights–I've probably had a legit "conversation" with ... all tolled ... maybe four or five strangers ever. Seriously. Single digits.

Which makes the story of how I met Corey Stiles all the more remarkable.

We were on a Southwest Airlines flight from Washington Dulles to Denver sitting window and aisle in 9A and 9C (if you've ever flown Southwest you know there's no business class available–but the closest thing to an "upgrade" is when there's nobody in the dreaded middle seat.) So the first icebreaker in this conversation between perfect strangers was a celebration of not having to endure being squeezed on both sides by some former Nebraska interior lineman in 9B – which was mercifully empty as we pushed back from the gate.

We then got on to "what do you do for a living?" only to discover that we each share the experience of writing a book. Of course, we were compelled (as if by literary law) to ask each other "*sooooo, what's YOUR book about*"– (I write about how companies can improve their customer service).

But even in her 30 second, courteously minimal synopsis, I knew that what this perfect stranger was telling me–the story of this book–was the single worst story I would ever imagine.

Of all the "stuff" one might go through in *this crazy life*–the amazing highlight-reel moments of your youth, your family events, your career accomplishments, all the good stuff, as well as the badness that happens from time to time: having a bone broken, having your heart broken, being in the wrong place at the wrong time, watching helplessly as people you love suffers from disease or misfortune–out of ALL the things that could even *conceivably* happen in the span of one's entire life ...

... there couldn't possibly be anything worse than the experience the woman in 9A was telling me about...in her short, 30 second story.

The story of losing a teenaged child.

Think about it: Right at that exact moment when you start to see your child–your offspring–as a true person, coming of age; full of unearned confidence, and untapped emotions, and exuberant irrationality,

beginning to achieve their first ever grown up victories–
right at the exact moment when you start to barely make
out the earliest light of your child's transition into self-
sufficiency…

… their light is extinguished. Like THAT.

Ya know…most of us parents get lucky (our son is now
23). Because for all the stupid hi-jinx kids get into, all the
juvenile growing-up awkwardness and horrible decision-
making of teenage-hood– somehow, they survive it all.

But here's this stranger in the window seat who did not
get lucky in that way.

What's the phrase we always use when we speak in polite
conversation about some teenaged kid suddenly dying?

They were so full of life

As I was listened, I was experiencing an emotional
reaction that I did NOT expect. Again, if I'm being honest,
I didn't even EXPECT to be talking to anyone on this flight.
Except maybe listening to 70's rock ballads too loud on my
earbuds and zoning out for the span of a few states.

And yet, here's this lady that I do not know, telling me
about an experience so painful that it's literally unthinkable.

Except I AM thinking about it.

Maybe I was nodding encouragingly, and maybe I was
trying to be a responsive listener, and maybe the words
coming out of my mouth were some conversational blah-blah
like. "*Wow … I can't even imagine,*" but what I was **feeling**…

….was kind of a cold-cocked, mule kick in the gut,
knockout blow to the soul.

Right there, across the empty middle seat, I truly believe
(at least for a brief moment in time) I could feel what SHE
must have felt – something like the physical inability to ever

draw breath again – following the worst phone call a parent could ever get.

But as she told me the details of her story, and as I started to better understand the genesis of her mission to help other people who have been through similar experiences, here's the thing that blew me away the most:

As horrible as this must be for any parent, what happened to Corey – losing her teenaged daughter in a car wreck – in fact, happens to a surprising and alarming number of families *every day*.

And if it's not a young woman, it's a young man. And if it's not a car crash, it's a bullet. Or (statistically slightly more likely) an empty pill bottle rolling out of a cold hand or a shower rod used in the most immodest way.

In the decade or so since Corey's daughter was killed, in the U.S. alone, tens of thousands of young people between the ages of 15-24 die suddenly. And, of course, that means there are now hundreds of thousands of family members who must somehow find some way to carry on afterward.

Perhaps **you** are one of those people.

If so, what you've experienced – at least in my mind, sitting here in the aisle seat - does not seem possible to survive. I doubt whether I could.

And yet, it is. It happened. To YOU of all people.

So what the hell are you supposed to do NOW?

I sincerely hope **this book** is YOUR "what now".

While there couldn't possibly be one "right way" you're supposed to live the rest of your days after the sudden death of a young adult–*frankly it would be insulting for anyone to tell you that there is*–what you will discover in the succeeding chapters is an assortment of the essential ingredients you will need to stock up on, in order to continue your own journey forward on the path of your own life.

It's all been carefully selected and curated by someone whose journey in *her* life is to help those who aren't exactly sure WHAT they're gonna need to survive at this point in *their* lives.

Each chapter offers an idea or suggestion worthy of your consideration. Of the things you like, take some and put 'em in your basket. Sure, you probably won't choose everything on every shelf, and likely you'll want to come up with your own proportions for each ingredient in your recipe. But you are welcome to push your basket down the aisle of each chapter, and take as much of each thing as you think you're gonna need.

Based on what you've been through already - and what you're likely to continue going through for the remainder of your time on this side - you're probably gonna need plenty.

But luckily, you've come to the right place.

Everything you're gonna need is right here.

—**Rick DeLisi**

Co-Author *"The Effortless Experience"*

CEB/Penguin Books

www.effortless-experience.com/

Mr. DeLisi works as a Principal Advisor for CEB, the global best-practice research firm located in Washington, DC. He is a noted keynote speaker, and has led executive briefings and seminars at locations around the world. His book The Effortless Experience *(co-authored with Matt Dixon and Nick Toman) is considered one of the most impactful works of the past few years on the subject of improving customer service.*

Introduction

Reviresco! I flourish again.
— Maxwell Clan Motto

DO YOU REMEMBER WHEN it hit you? When you first heard the news? Can you go back to the second day? The third week? The fourth month? Even as I write this, twelve years later, when I go back and remember these points in time I feel the heaviness in my gut. My heart beats faster. My shoulders slump. My breath becomes shallow and swift.

Whether grief shocked you out of a normal routine or you watched it approach, when it hits, when you get the news of finality, you are instantly consumed by a dark, cold, and wet storm of emotions, thoughts, physical sensations, and shattered dreams that dominate your senses and your life.

I remember being incredibly disoriented. Prior to that moment, my life felt like a high-speed train zipping along the tracks of life with joy, meaning, and enthusiasm. In the days and weeks following Aleisha's accident, I would see the sun shine, watch cars racing along the streets, observe people going about their lives in that same high-speed manner and think that I should be in that momentum too. But my life train had been stopped in its tracks in an unfamiliar landscape. I felt like I was halted in the middle of a rickety railway bridge, in treacherous mountain terrain. I couldn't wrap my head around it.

After the year of firsts, and as time moved on, the waves of shock grew further apart. But when they did hit, I experienced the disorientation and the disbelief all over again. Even now, twelve years later, I will occasionally get hit with "an Aleisha moment" and find myself in the dark, now-familiar landscape of grief. It is a generally accepted notion that once the year of firsts has passed, it's time to begin to rebuild your life and re-identify yourself. That's easier said than done, and for many people it's just easier to stay on the fragile raft of sorrow.

MY STORY/ALEISHA'S STORY

My journey into the hollows of grief began on a bright, crisp fall morning in October 2004, my favorite time of year. I was driving home from church, mentally planning the events of the coming week. Aleisha called me as she was leaving her friend's house, where she had spent the night. They were on their way to try out a new church and she invited me to join them and then go shopping afterwards. I declined and, being the mom, reminded her that she needed to write her essay for her pending scholarship application. She assured me she was on top of it. We both ended our call with, "I love you!"

Not more than five minutes later I walked in the door of my home to find my husband Kevin on the phone, sounding alarmed. I heard him say, "Did you call 911?" As he came up the stairs he said, "Aleisha's been hit. We need to go." The shock and disorientation was instant and overwhelming. I had just spoken to her. We didn't know what condition she was in.

We jumped in the car and raced to the scene of the accident, about seven miles from our house. As we pulled up we could see her car smashed on the driver's side, lots of emergency vehicles, and, a bit further beyond, a semi-tractor trailer askew across the road. The heaviness from my heart to my gut felt like a hundred cinder blocks. Breathing was difficult.

Aleisha's friend was beside herself as she relayed the events she had witnessed in her rearview mirror. Aleisha, following her friend on their way to church, was making a left turn onto a two-lane highway. She apparently didn't see the semi barreling down on her at about 55 mph. There was no time for him to stop and he broadsided her driver's side.

Shortly after we arrived the EMT came over and informed us that they were working on her, but it didn't look good. I felt nauseous, I think I might have screamed, I was oh so cold. I was overwhelmed with the most intense fear I had ever known. I was in utter disbelief that this could be happening because I had just spoken to her.

In the midst of my confusion and fear I distinctly remember having enough lucidity to know that if this was it, if it was her soul's mission to leave this planet, I wanted her to KNOW she was loved. I never prayed for her to stay, though with every fiber of my being that's what I wanted. Instead, I kept repeating over and over, "I love you, Aleisha! I love you, Aleisha!" If she was leaving the planet I wanted her to feel my love going with her.

A few minutes later, Flight for Life left the scene. The EMT came over to us and with tears in her eyes told us that they had done everything they could. I did what any mother would do... I screamed.

The next few hours were a blur as my husband and teenage son and I returned home, and people started arriving. I distinctly remember the utter disbelief of having to share the news with family and friends. The shock to us as a family, to our community, was immense. I still remember the first words and reactions of most people. Some responses were loving and compassionate. Others were shockingly cold. As the condolences and remembrances began to pour in we learned how great Aleisha's impact was in the world. To this day, we hear stories from people who never knew her but who are inspired by her life.

THE EARLY WEEKS AND MONTHS OF GRIEF

As I embarked on this unwanted journey through grief, I found myself faced with decisions that I couldn't believe I was having to make. Looking back now, I can see the organization, the purpose, and the symbolism in some of these events. The following were key messages and events that were fundamental to my grieving process in both the early days and in the years to follow.

- ▶ Our dear friend Kevin, who had the incredible capacity to hold vast spiritual space for us, said on the day of Aleisha's accident, "You're under an umbrella of grace now."
- ▶ One of Aleisha's teachers took us aside and counseled us to allow each other to grieve differently because we each had a different relationship with her.
- ▶ The same wise friend from above also gently reminded us, "You know, on some level, you agreed to this."
- ▶ One week after her death, we attended the ballet — on Halloween night!

- ▶ Two weeks after her accident we went on a cruise with her boyfriend's family.
- ▶ Approximately one month after we attended an animated movie — *The Incredibles.*
- ▶ Now, I realize that Aleisha's mission in this life was complete... and mine is not!

Choosing to participate in some these pre-planned events turned out to be meaningful activities that honored Aleisha's playful energy and her love of friends, family, and fun. She danced ballet for many years and had a deep love and respect for the art. Kevin and I barely remember the ballet that Halloween night, as we cried through most of it. Aleisha had been looking forward to the cruise for months. While the decision to go ahead on the cruise was excruciating, it gave all of us a chance to grieve privately and deeply for a focused and finite period of time. We didn't stop grieving when we returned home, but it helped provide some structure around the depth of grief.

The only time I was ever mad was when we went to see *The Incredibles*. I could not believe I was participating in something So Silly, So Mundane, So Insignificant... until I remembered how much Aleisha would have loved this movie and laughed through it. I'm not sure I allowed myself to actually laugh during that movie, but I did begin to allow the idea of laughter, of joy, of the HaPpY Aleisha legacy to bud in the darkness of my sorrow.

In retrospect, I can appreciate the messages from others who, in those early days, were able to hold more neutral space for us with wise, loving arms. These messages became guidelines for daily life as we navigated the early stages of grief. I would literally imagine an umbrella of grace being held over my husband, my son and me by a divine being. It was a comfort.

We three remaining family members consciously moved into a relationship of deep respect with one another as we allowed each other to grieve in our own unique way. We would check in with each other, we talked about her when we felt like it, and we navigated grief according to our respective relationships with Aleisha. We continue this today. We recognize that each of us had a different relationship with Aleisha that would dictate diverse journeys of grief.

Perhaps the most stunning and difficult to digest message was, "On some level you agreed to this." I know! I KNOW! Even now, as I write that, MY "inner lizard" (that critical, doubtful voice in the mind) of fear and disbelief is raging a battle cry within. "Are you freaking kidding me?!?!" she's screaming. "I did NOT agree to this. And if by some feat of crazy arrangement, I DID, I rescind that agreement!!! I want her back – NOW!"

I get that the idea of a soul agreement is powerful and may seem utterly impossible. And yet, it has become perhaps the most comforting of all. We want an explanation, a justification for WHY this happened to us, to our son or daughter. Logically, there isn't one. To me this state of soul agreement is far more comforting than some of the other platitudes I've heard and that clients of mine have heard, like:

▶ *She's in a better place.* – Ugh! – Insert massive eye roll here.
▶ *God wanted/needed him.* – Ugh! Ugh! Ugh! – God has an inexhaustible resource of souls.
▶ *At least she's not in pain and suffering anymore.* – Okay, true. But other people with her condition have pulled through, why not her?
▶ *He's happy now, Earth was just too hard for him.* Again, true, but I was still hopeful he would pull out of his depression.

The following were the only explanations I could receive. I think I could hear them because they made me think beyond the classic clichés and in a strange, rather esoteric way, gave me a snippet of control.

▶ On some level you agreed to this. (Shared by my friend Kevin)

▶ Her mission in this life was complete. (My own discernment)

The point in extracting an explanation is to give us a starting point, to show us a way to bring the broken, disconnected pieces of our mental and emotional spirits together so that we can carry on with our own life mission.

In the last twelve years, dozens of people have come to me to share their stories of grief and loss. Without exception they are looking for a way to live again. They want to know how I've done it. Many have asked me to write a book and me, being a classic resister, well... I resisted!

Why did I resist? Because I haven't done anything earth-shattering. My journey hasn't changed the face of grief or altered the classic steps of the grieving process. Truth be told, I didn't even follow those steps. So I didn't really think I had anything to share. In fact, even when my publisher strongly encouraged me to write about this topic, I balked! I resisted again! I couldn't get off the phone with her fast enough when she brought it up. I was speechless and needed to sit with this idea. I've learned that my resistance is a way for me to stall until I have time to think about an idea or a request a little bit more information. So I got out my yoga mat and I moved my body and I sat in stillness, allowing the idea to incubate.

What emerged from my incubation time is that my journey, my tools, and my techniques may not be rocket science or revolutionary. The practices that led me out of grief and into joy were heavily influenced by other teachers, belief systems, and modalities that weren't specifically focused on grief. The most meaningful and helpful practices for me were regular yoga sessions, learning to breathe again through various techniques, plenty of time in nature, meditations and sound vibrations, and more. My methods were SIMPLE and easily accessible to me at any point in time. And though they may seem a bit elementary, especially to those who have walked a dedicated spiritual path, they worked to help me slowly begin to heal, to reclaim my identity and my joy, and to create a new normal life that I love. And I believe these simple steps can help others.

My journey of healing, hope, and joy has been propelled by the wisdom of teachers, authors, musicians and sages. Even though I've never met many of them, THEY have held space for my healing heart. They have guided me directly and indirectly through their teachings, prayers, music, and rituals. On these pages you will find some things that are my own original ideas. There are several tools, gleaned from master teachers and coaches, that I have tweaked to address the grieving mother's heart. I share many techniques, as authentically as my middle-aged brain can recall learning them. It is these techniques, which I have practiced over and over for years, that have helped me sculpt a new life. My deepest gratitude to these masters who have influenced me. And my sincerest apologies for any misrepresentation of your work.

YOUR STORY

YOUR STORY MAY BE SIMILAR or completely different. Where we connect is likely in the shock and the overwhelming nature of grief. Looking back over the months and years since you began your journey through grief, I'm sure you remember the most unusual things. Perhaps you see signs that allow you to make a modicum of sense about what's happened. Do you sometimes find yourself disoriented and in disbelief, still?

Grief like yours can be all-consuming. It can overpower you so that your daily experience is like living in a constant storm of darkness, heaviness, sorrow, apathy, and fear. Grief shocks you into a new pattern of living, and for many people this gloomy, weighted sadness becomes a way of life.

I believe wholeheartedly, my dearest reader, that you too can carve a new, meaningful way of living out of the dark heaviness of your grief. I am standing beside you, virtually cheering your progress. Imagine that you have a friend, a guide who understands your pain and your despair, who is holding the vision of *your new life of joy* as you take your first steps.

TWO IMPORTANT CONCEPTS

BEFORE MOVING ON, I WANT share two important concepts:

1. **Death is NOT a failure!** In our culture, death is the ultimate failure. I feel for physicians who must deal with this on a regular basis. Their ultimate mission and all of their training is designed to save and prolong lives. When someone dies, many doctors feel they have failed. But there is always a subtle, invisible soul intention behind the life of the patient that goes unaccounted for. Regardless of how your loved one moved on from this realm, please allow space in your being for the belief that death is not a failure. There is SO MUCH MORE beyond this physical incarnation.

You may not be able to make cognitive sense of it right now, but allow a pinpoint of belief to take hold in your mind. Repeat this statement to yourself to allow the notion to take root and grow.

2. **Love NEVER dies!** Love is an energy that is more powerful than our fear and our grief. It is the gift of Spirit to us in a never-ending flow. When our loved one dies that energy of love between us continues. It does not cease. And though they have transitioned to a nonphysical realm, they too are continuing to pour that energy of love into us. They show us in SO many ways via signs, symbols, and synchronistic messages. WE fail to receive it due to the antics of disbelief in the mind. Stop the resistance, my friend, and allow the love to nourish your aching heart and weary mind.

You can begin now to use those two statements as mantras to initiate your journey to joy.

HOW TO GET THE MOST FROM THIS BOOK

THIS GUIDE IS SORT OF like a retreat in a book. It is really about extreme self-care and nurturing. Most of the techniques can be easily modified to make them personal to you. Again, imagine you have someone by your side who truly understands you. Together we will laugh, cry, and scream over the past. We will pray, meditate, move, and breathe in the present. And we will imagine a new identity and new normal for the future.

This guide is intended primarily for those who have passed the Year of Firsts – first Thanksgiving, first Christmas, first birthday, first Mother's Day. The Year of Firsts is its own journey and requires different attention and respect.

You will get the most out of this book if you are willing and open to:

- ▶ Being happy again
- ▶ Changing your mind (aka re-patterning your thoughts)
- ▶ Loving your body and moving it
- ▶ Going into and trusting your feelings
- ▶ Believing in the power of your soul's purpose for your life
- ▶ Having hope
- ▶ Taking responsibility for your life

If you feel a strong resistance to any of these notions you will likely have a difficult time with the rest of the content contained here. That's ok. The time isn't right and/or this isn't the best fit for your personal belief system. This book does not talk about the classic Five Stages of Grief. I didn't follow those stages and several of the other mothers in grief I know did not follow those stages. In addition, this book doesn't adhere to any specific religious or philosophical belief system. There are contributions from MANY inspirational sources.

I've worked with dozens of people who are in various stages of grief. This is a simple, self-nurturing path that has a unique and magical way of bringing about healing and creating the space to allow you to reclaim your joy.

I'm glad YOU are here!

"Honor the space between no longer and not yet."
— Nancy Levin

CHAPTER 1
Pleasure vs. Pain

Be not the slave of your moods, but their master. But if you are so angry, so depressed
and so sore that your spirit cannot find deliverance and peace even in prayer, then quickly
go and give some pleasure to someone lowly or sorrowful, or to a guilty or innocent
sufferer. Sacrifice yourself, your talent, your time, your rest to another, to one who has
to bear a heavier load than you – and your unhappy mood will dissolve into a blessed,
contented submission to God. – Abdu'l-Baha

IN A FEW MOMENTS WE'LL JUMP into my tips for
reclaiming your joy. But first it's important to set the tone
and lay a foundation that will allow you to be fully present
as you engage in this deep inner work. The practices contained
in this book are very simple tools that I have used myself and
have taught others to use. What I know to be true is that grief
can be all-consuming, and short, simple, accessible methods
are more readily integrated into your daily life than long
explanations and complicated methodologies. These rituals
may seem overly simplistic but that is the brilliance of them.
They quietly work their transformational magic in your life.

CREATE YOUR SPACE

To begin, create a sacred space where you can feel
comfortable, be alone, and feel safe to explore yourself deeply
without the inhibitions of being in the company of others.

This is YOUR journey. Not your spouse's, girlfriends', other children's, etc. The only exception to this rule of solitude is a beloved pet. Our canine and feline kids have a unique quality of being able to hold and nurture sacred space.

You might consider setting up an altar of sorts where you place special, powerful, meaningful items in a place of honor and in your natural line of sight. This also helps to foster the sacredness of the space and your journey.

To the best of your ability, try to use tools that speak to all of the five senses. For instance, comfortable, soft clothing for the skin and maybe some hand cream nearby. Soft music or an open window to hear the birds sing, the mountain wind whispering through the trees, or the soothing rhythm of the waves. Be near a window, on your patio, on a bench in a park, or at the beach. In other words, someplace where you can *see* nature. Light a candle and/or use a white sage smudging stick to set the scent vibration for your olfactory sense. Finally, have some indulgence for your taste buds at the ready. Tea, mints, and chocolate are a great place to start. However, keep it light. We're not looking for a full meal here, just a bit of taste.

Journaling is a great way to help clear space in the mind. Water, coffee, or tea are good to have nearby as well as lots of tissues. You might like to have a photo of you, your family, your departed son or daughter. What you DON'T need for your trek is your cell phone, your home phone, your computer, or tablet. Set those aside for now. Give yourself the gift of time. This is YOUR healing journey. Honor it.

It's a good idea to establish the sacredness of your space with a prayer, meditation, intention, a song, or a chant. We will discuss this in more detail later. For now, make it something short, simple, and meaningful for you.

DISCONNECTED FROM PLEASURE

WHEN WE SPEND AN EXTENDED period of time in grief we lose our connection with pleasure. I've noticed that those who get stuck in the quicksand of sorrow have forgotten what pleasure feels like. Even extracting a simple smile from them is a major feat. Allowing pleasure to take residence in you again is fundamental to reclaiming your joy and moving into a new normal life. The quickest way to begin experiencing pleasure again is via the senses. As mothers, many of us have lost touch with what feels pleasurable, as we have sacrificed our needs and desires for those of our kids. This was a no-brainer. We were happy to do it. But this pattern of ignoring our needs adds additional suffering when we are consumed with grief.

A couple of scenarios can arise from this additional suffering. First, because we are so used to neglecting our needs and feelings, when bombarded with the overwhelming emotions of grief we stuff our feelings and ignore our experience to become the comforter of everyone in the family and/or community. In short, we keep mothering and continue overlooking ourselves. The second scenario of additional suffering comes from fueling our agony with the martyr or victim syndrome. We literally use our grief as an excuse to stay powerless, helpless, sad, and inert. Both of these scenarios keep us in a pattern of pain either through avoidance or conscious suffering. The idea of self- nurturing and pleasure is completely foreign. And we fail to see how it will lift us out of the comfort zone of grief that we have established.

Because of our history of ignoring our feelings, needs, and desires, it is almost universal for mothers in grief to become disconnected with their experience of pleasure when completely saturated with pain. In addition, society adds its burden of guilt on us by silently inferring that, while we should move on, we definitely should not experience pleasure.

At this point in your journey through the hollows of grief, you have likely experienced one or possibly all of these scenarios:

▶ You're completely numb (or close to it) and simply going through the motions of life with no interest, enthusiasm, or motivation.
▶ You're overly busy to avoid feeling anything.
▶ You've had snippets of happiness, hilarity, or laughter and shut them down because how can you possibly be happy? But you may have noticed that it feels oh-so-good to laugh again!

As I've already mentioned, grief can become all-consuming. It literally takes over your thoughts. Sadness demands FULL occupancy of your heart. Your body may still be holding on to the energy of the shock, in addition to holding the energy of the ongoing emotions. And your spirit? What spirit? you may say. I have a spirit? What is that? In other words, you're totally disconnected from it.

A significant part of your soul's intention for this life is to partake in pleasure and joy. This is the desire of every soul incarnating on Earth. Our souls also desire to grow and learn from the challenges we experience in life. As you may be experiencing, some life challenges cause you to evade the vast array of pleasures that make up life on Earth.

In a few moments we're going to explore what YOU find pleasurable from the perspective of each of your senses. But first, let's establish a standard by which you can assess your experience of pain and pleasure in any given moment.

TIP #1: CULTIVATE MORE PLEASURE

IMAGINE A SCALE FROM NEGATIVE 10 to positive 10. Negative 10 represents the most excruciating event you've ever experienced. Positive 10 represents the most pleasurable moment in your life.

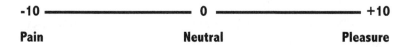

Take a moment and think about a time in your life when you experienced heartbreaking pain. Most likely the most powerful experience of heartbreaking pain was the death of your child. You can use that experience or another one. Let yourself remember that event as fully as possible. Give the emotions permission to rise up; notice any physical sensations in the body. Allow yourself a few moments to deeply feel that experience of pain. Imagine the scene, hear the sounds, take note of any smells. Notice any thoughts and/or the fight-or-flight response activating. Now take several deep breaths – and with each exhalation, release that energy out of your body. LET IT GO! Take a sip of water. Eat some chocolate.

Now go back in your memory and relive a moment when you experienced great pleasure. Pick a time when you felt euphoric, blissful, or good in your body. Maybe you were laughing hysterically at something. Or maybe in the throes of passion. Allow as much of this emotional energy to move through your body as you can. Give yourself permission to *feel* this pleasurable experience as intensely as possible. Now, again, take a few cleansing breaths to neutralize your body, mind, and emotions before moving on.

We have now established YOUR Pleasure and Pain Scale (P/P Scale). Again, negative 10 represents the most painful experience in your life and positive 10 represents a time when you experienced extreme pleasure. You can play with the different points between zero and negative 10 and zero and positive 10. For "extra credit," you can take the time to identify what each of those points are on the scale. It's optional.

Now, using the P/P Scale, let's get into some new experiences of pleasure.

THE POWER OF THE SENSES

OUR BODIES HAVE BEEN BRILLIANTLY designed to participate in pleasure via the five senses. Each of our senses is an invitation to activate our playful nature and participate in decadent sense-ful (sensual) experiences to bring texture, color, and harmony to our lives. Allowing ourselves to indulge in pleasure brings a balancing effect to the stresses of life such as the demands of work, family obligations, community expectations and... the anxiety of grief.

Grief draws attention completely away from pleasure. In addition to being disorienting and all-consuming, grief is depleting. Even now, a year or two into the grief, you may still find that you have no energy available except the energy to be sad, depressed, or inert. These energies are heavy and lead to easily getting stuck in the dark storm of sorrow.

Our five senses are the body's way of assessing and categorizing pain and pleasure. Benjamin Franklin said, "Tell me and I'll forget. Show me and I might remember. Involve me and I'll understand." Increasing your awareness of pleasure through experience or involvement is the best way to get simple ideas to make a lasting impact. Stimulation of your senses is available to you at any time and in any place to help you re-member what is pleasurable to YOU!

In a study on the power of the senses in commercial branding, Mail Media Centre of the UK stated this regarding the five senses:

Sight: 83% of all information we receive is visual. We will experience up to a 46 % increase in mood if we see a positive picture.

Smell: The sense of smell emotionally affects humans up to 75% more than any other sense!

Touch: Our mood will increase by up to 29% if we are exposed to positive tactile feeling.

Taste: Our mood will increase by up to 23% if we are exposed to a positive taste.

Sound: Positive sound will increase our mood by up to 65%.

Imagine the shift in your life if you were to begin a practice of *focusing more on what feels good* than concentrating on the pain of your sorrow. Let's focus on your senses right now, exactly where you're at.

Sight is the sense that we rely on the most. Mentally we more readily find words to describe what we see than any other sense. Stop right now and look around you. If you're inside, look out the window. What do you see? From where you sit right now, what is the most pleasurable thing within your line of sight? Walk around your home (inside and out) and find places that speak to you in a positive way. If you find pleasurable visual stimulation lacking, make a note of it and set an intention to purchase a picture, blow up and frame an old photograph, buy a plant, or paint a room. Set an intention to bring more positive visual stimulation into your life.

Make a note of the visual pleasure your get from your home, your walks, your neighborhood, your community, etc. When you have an actual list on hand, it will serve you when the going gets rough. Your journal will become your go-to guide when you need to literally get back on track to joy.

Smell is the most powerful of the senses. It's linked to the emotions, sexuality, and drive. Smell is the sense that stimulates memory. In addition, it is through the sense of smell that we get to experience all the delicious flavors of life. It is the aroma of our food that activates our taste buds and digestive juices. Imagine, right now, the smell of a freshly sliced lemon. Can you feel your nostrils opening up? Maybe you're even salivating a bit. What is your favorite aroma from childhood? Baking bread, chocolate chip cookies, the pine scent of a Christmas tree, maybe your grandmother's perfume? Pause here and go on an olfactory exploration. Find candles, spices, perfumes that make you feel safe, happy, secure, loved. WRITE THEM DOWN. Start an aroma list. You'll want to refer back to this list on your journey to joy.

Touch: When I was in college, studying to become an elementary school teacher, I learned that the human being needs eight hugs a day to thrive. Generally, as a society, we are so out of touch with tactile stimulation. I know people who can't stand to be touched and while I respect their wishes, I ache for them. It is common knowledge that babies who are held and cuddled regularly are generally healthier. The benefits of hugging are:

▶ Improves immune function
▶ Lowers heart rate
▶ Boosts oxytocin levels, which impacts the emotional center of the brain and promotes contentment while reducing anxiety
▶ Increases feeling of security and trust
▶ Teaches us the benefits of both giving and receiving
▶ Stimulates serotonin, which helps alleviate loneliness and depression

If hugging is uncomfortable for you, massage is another great way to receive touch in a professionally respectful way. A few days after Aleisha passed away, someone gifted me a Grief Massage. It was the first time this massage therapist had been asked to perform such a massage. He showed up with just the right nurturing touch, quiet presence, and respectful energy. He allowed me to cry, to be silent, to be. I have a couple of friends who remember Aleisha's hugs, and every time we see each other we consciously engage in hugging one another the way she did. To this day, I am a hugger. It benefits both me and the one on the receiving end. This may be the most challenging of the senses for you to find pleasure in. Explore this. Alone. With your partner. With a beloved friend. It's a good idea to remember to breathe when exploring the tactile sense to help relieve excess anxiety about being touched. If you simply can't engage in physical contact with another human being, I strongly encourage you to explore other tactile pleasures. Soft fabrics. Touching, cuddling, or caressing a pet. Norfolk pine trees! Your body is covered with skin that is highly sensitive. Feed that sensitivity in a way that brings you comfort, makes you feel safe, and elevates your mood.

Taste is the least effective of our five senses. It is highly individual. Every person has a different number of taste receptors on their tongue, which gives each of us varying degrees of intensity for the different flavors. For instance, someone who is sensitive to salt has MORE salt receptors on their tongue than someone who adds salt to everything. As seen from the brand impact list above, taste only has a 23% improvement impact on our mood. Sooo why then do some of us self-medicate with food? Remember, there is a strong connection between smell and taste. And smell activates our memories. I would venture here that taste, enhanced by smell, reinforces memory activation, which for many of us is a comforting experience. We smell food, then we taste it as we eat to feel better. Comfort food, anyone? Even though the sense of taste has a low-impact rate, food, meals, and dining are some of the most pleasurable experiences we have. Consider all the holidays we celebrate that are centered around food. When we are dating we often go out for a nice dinner and a movie. To celebrate life's milestones – birthdays, anniversaries, graduations, weddings – we celebrate with food. FOOD IS PLEASURE!

To bring this sense into greater consciousness, write down your favorite comfort foods. List your favorite meals, holiday celebrations, dinner date locations. Go on a culinary exploration in your kitchen! Pull out some of your favorite foods to sample from a pleasure perspective. Ask yourself why you like this particular food. Is it the texture, the flavor, the aroma, the memory? When we grieve we subconsciously seek relief. Food is easily accessible and eating is perhaps the most accepted form of pleasure in our culture. Self-medicating with food during the grieving process is quite normal. To prevent this from getting out of control, spend time thinking about what you are eating and why it feels comforting to you. Does it trigger a memory of safety, love, well-being?

Sound is one of the senses that we can't control. Touch is the other one. We can't close our ears. We can't turn off our skin. When our ears work, we hear! The only way to shut out sound is to use earplugs. Some work, some don't. For many people, being in a completely sound-proof room is a bit disconcerting. We are used to having auditory stimulation all the time. Even people who live in the mountains or out in the country have nature sounds that keep their hearing alert. Sound can activate emotions in a powerful way. A sure-fire trigger into a puddle of tears for me is music. I can't tell you the number of times I've been shopping and could not escape the music in the store or even outside between stores. When that trigger occurs, I simply allow it to be, trusting that it's time again for another tearful release. Hearing recordings of Aleisha's laughter will lift me up rather than send me spiraling downward.

Sound, especially music, can ignite feelings of falling in love. Falling in love with nature, with another person, with a child, with a pet... with yourself. You probably already have certain styles of music that you listen to, to energize you. Some music makes you introspective and/or melancholy. Other forms of music can cause you to relax. When listening to music do you prefer the deep, low beat of a drum or bass guitar? Or would you find more pleasure in a lilting flute or singing violin? Maybe it's the warmth of acoustic guitar that you love or the brightness of piano. What about nature? What are your favorite sounds in nature? Explore your sound preferences and again ask yourself why you like these particular sounds. How do these sounds help you to experience pleasure? Chart your auditory preferences on your P/P Scale.

This excursion into your senses is intended to reacquaint you with what feels good to YOU – no *shoulding* allowed! Decide now, my friend, to allow more pleasure into your life via your five senses. I'm not saying eliminate the sadness. Allow it. When sorrow surfaces, allow those emotions to bubble up. Feel them. Be gentle, loving, and accepting of your heart and body in holding those emotions until you feel ready to look at them and release them... again and again and again. The idea here is simply to bring greater awareness to when and where you experience pleasure and to cultivate more of that.

Ginger Tea for Grief

Years ago I read that ginger tea helps you move through the grieving process. I don't know if it's true, but ginger does help tremendously with digestion, relieves nausea, and boosts the immune system. A local Thai restaurant where I live makes the most soothing warm ginger tea. Here's the recipe as I remember it:

Warm Ginger Tea

> 1 piece fresh ginger, peeled and sliced
> Brown sugar to taste
> Lemon juice, optional
> Water

Start with 1 to 1 1/2 cups of water. Use more to dilute as necessary. Place sliced ginger and water in a saucepan. Bring water to boil. Reduce heat and add brown sugar, one teaspoon at a time, tasting as you go. Simmer for

15 minutes. Stir lemon juice in for the last 5 minutes of simmering. Strain liquid into a cup. Dilute with additional water as needed.

I've assembled a variety of tips in a neat little package just for you. I call it the Reclaim Your Joy Toolkit. Visit griefinterruptedbook.com.

CHAPTER 2
Let Nature Soften You

When we enter into ritual we strengthen our connection with the cycles of nature.
It brings us into rhythm with the natural world and with our own nature. When we
take time to step outside of the mundane world, we encounter the rich flow of
spiritual energy.... Entering sacred space helps us awaken
to what is eternal within ourselves. — *Sandra Kynes,* A Year of Ritual

I HAVE WORKED WITH MANY clients over the years
to help them recover from various stresses and traumas by
establishing simple rituals that allow them to reconnect with
the pulse of joy within their hearts. One of my coaching
clients, Karen, is a physician with a busy practice spanning
two offices. She has a young family with three children
who are active in multiple activities. She rarely sleeps a
full night. As a physician who loses patients and has to
deliver distressing news to family members, Karen carries
a stress load that many of us would wilt under. Karen has
two rituals that she regularly engages in that get her out
in nature. These are practices she indulges in regularly to
keep her sane, calm, and inspired. First, when it rains, she
goes out in the hospital parking and skips! This reconnects
her to her playful side and gives her a much needed energy
boost to make it through the rest of her day. Her second
self-nurturing practice is simply sitting on a nearby beach
for a minimum of thirty minutes twice a week. Sometimes

she takes her kids along and lets them play in the water or hunt for sea glass while she allows the rhythm of the waves to nurture her weary soul. Karen knows, from years of engaging in these rituals, that they help her be a better physician and a more attentive and patient mother. She also sleeps better and experiences a greater sense of well-being.

THE HEALING PULSE OF NATURE

Nature is your constant ally in life. From the flora and fauna of where you live to the weather patterns and the wildlife, nature is speaking to you always. Sometimes her message is subtle; other times she rages with wind, storms, or intense heat. Nature invites us to participate *with* her rather than against her. When we disrespect her, she lets us know. The Earth is our true home in this life. And home is a comfort in challenging times. Many of us are so busy in our lives that we completely ignore the beauty, the peace, and the healing vibration of the natural world around us.

Many cultures through the eons of time have used ritual, ceremonies, and symbols from nature to bring peace, calm, and a sense of well-being to people. The quote above reminds us that regular communion with nature connects us to the pulse of the planet. When we pause to interact with nature, we generally move into a more appreciative relationship with her. This improved bond brings a quietude, especially to the emotions. The energy of nature sort of reaches out and draws erratic emotional energy into vibrational alignment. In addition, nature has a mystical way of calming racing thoughts that tend to aggravate the emotions. Combined, these two benefits generally leave the individual feeling composed and the sympathetic nervous system more settled.

TIP #2: LET NATURE SOFTEN YOU

When was the last time you spent an hour or more outside or even sitting by a window? What rituals do you have that allow you to interact with nature and use all of your senses?

As I write to you I am sitting at a desk looking out over a valley with a mountain on the other side. There's a gorgeous pine tree just outside my window, which is cracked open, and I can smell and feel the fresh mountain air coming through. A soft breeze is whispering through the pines and birds are going about their day with a song. It's October and the light has a soft golden glow. Ha! Just now a big gust came by and howled through the open window. I giggled and said hello to the wind.

Nature's healing effect softens the tension of extended grief and brings us back to center. It calms our nerves, boosts our mood, and leads us to a place of peace quicker than any other tool. You can't live vibrantly on this planet without interacting with nature.

> If we surrendered to the earth's intelligence we would rise up rooted like trees.
> — Rainier Maria Rilke

Whether you're on a mountain top, on the beach, or sitting on a bench in a park, nature has a grounding effect. It brings us into awareness of our senses. We have explored the five senses as a way to bring more pleasure into your life. We're trying to create a new pattern of cultivating more pleasure than pain as you go about your days. At this point, grief has likely taken over your awareness. Everything you experience is influenced by your sadness. This is normal. And now it's time for you to take yourself in hand and create ritual, fresh patterning, and a new normal life. We're taking simple steps to move away from pain and toward pleasure, hope, and joy. It's important to practice receiving and giving, playing in the world of pleasure as well as working at your craft every single day. Nature is a simple, reliable resource. If we allow her to, Mother Nature will envelope us in her branches of love, peace, and healing with consistency, with variety, and with humor. It's up to us to notice.

SEASONED WITH JOY

We can't talk about nature without talking about the seasons. My personal journey to joy was "seasoned" with ongoing permission slips from myself to feel pleasure again. When I say seasoned I mean adopting a heightened awareness of each season and immersing myself in it.

I love the varied energy, tone and ritual of each season, some more than others. I would travel the globe in perpetual autumn if I could.

In winter, on snowy days, the light is a peaceful, monochromatic hue. Though snow may be drifting all about, inside my canine kids are inviting me to rest with them in storm mode. Warm cups of tea, hearty soups and stews, sweaters, blankets, and couch cuddles are nurturing and warming to the soul. Winter reminds us to reflect internally and to rest from our labors of the previous harvest. But days of hibernation often lead to restlessness. And just about the time when you can't take another day of snow and cold....

Spring arrives! There are more daylight hours. The air is warmer and everything in nature turns a brilliant green as the trees, grass, and flowers renew with life. Springtime bulbs greet us with color after the blue-gray days of winter. Fresh asparagus and bright strawberries remind us to fuel ourselves from the earth. Spring is a time of hope and renewal of our vital energy.

As spring turns to summer we naturally move into a highly active state. Though many of us are no longer relying solely on our own land to feed us, we do enjoy gardening and other outdoor activities. The heat of summer gets us moving as we strive to soak up every hour of light. We are often more social in summer, investing in relationships with our community that will help keep us connected in the darker days of winter, via phone and social media.

The golden days of autumn typically reveal Mother Nature in her finest glory. The slanted light from the sun moving south illuminates the changing leaves with a rich, honeyed hue. The sky becomes an azure umbrella. Our autumnal rituals include raking and crunching leaves, numerous feast-filled holidays, a deep dive into gratitude, and pumpkins! Everything Pumpkin!

How can you turn up your attunement to the season you are currently in? What rituals are already in place in your life that you can participate in more mindfully? Using your P/P Scale, can you surrender to the energy of nature in your current season and allow that energy to reveal a new point of pleasure in your life?

Your grief will still be there. You can visit it any time you want. Just give it a finite amount of time because you've got some joy to be living in this season of your life.

CHAPTER 3

Reframe Your Storytelling

Progress is impossible without change and those who cannot change
their minds cannot change anything.— George Bernard Shaw

RECLAIMING YOUR JOY DOESN'T HAPPEN overnight.
It's a process of daily releasing debilitating grief energy and
willingly choosing joy over and over again. Establishing
a new normal requires you to own where you are in your
life right now. There is a magical liberation that takes place
when you take responsibility for where you are. Literally
anything becomes possible in that sphere of potentiality.
One of the challenges inherent with grief, though, is getting
overly entangled in self-pity. When you adopt the mantle
of the victim, you give your power away to everyone else,
making them responsible for your happiness and fulfillment
minute to minute. It's difficult not to feel sorry for yourself
when you lose a child. A short season of self-pity is definitely
part of the grieving process, but it must have an end date.
YOU have to pick yourself up and dust yourself off, and take
small action steps every single day to make joy and pleasure
tangible in your life again. The senses and the seasons are a
simple, easy place to begin.

Grief will always have a presence in your life. The idea is to make adjustments so that it doesn't consume you for the rest of your life. The gloom of sorrow provides the counterpoint for the luminosity of joy. It's vital for a sense of wholeness and well-being to embrace both the light and shadow aspects of your life experience. In this chapter we will discuss both, focusing for a time on the shadow aspect of self-pity.

My friend Lynelle lost her daughter to an overdose four years ago. Lynelle is surrounded by a large family, including a loving husband, her adult son, and three grandchildren. She has a rather comfortable life. Three times in the last year I have run into Lynelle while out shopping. Sometimes she is alone and sometimes she is with her husband. Every time I see her, her eyes are dull and downcast. If I run into her when she is alone, she will inevitably launch into a saga about all the awful things that are going on in her life and how unhappy she is with everyone around her. When I inquire about her son and husband, she has a difficult time relating anything positive about them. Often I'll probe more in an attempt to bring some joy and light into her awareness. She usually sighs and proceeds to tell me everything that is wrong in her life. When I try to turn her around to something positive or joyful, she has a difficult time stepping into that sphere of awareness. If I happen to run into her while she is with her husband, she clams up and lets him do all the talking. He almost always describes what a difficult time Lynelle is having. I have reached out to Lynelle numerous times to meet for tea but she always declines, saying she just doesn't feel up to it. Her husband would love to have his wife back to engage in life again; her grandchildren are bright lights that could illuminate the dark corners and bring a potent experience of pleasure into her daily life. But Lynelle is still very anchored in her grief. She has become used to getting attention from her family for being the grieving mother. She's not quite ready *yet* to step onto the path toward joy. I have faith that she will find her path to joy soon.

LIGHT AND SHADOW ASPECTS OF YOUR MIND

The mind is your conscious control center. Like the emotions, it has both light and shadow aspects. The mind can raise you up with inspiring visions or tear you down with worrisome rhetoric. Your thoughts can trigger emotions that cause you to leap forward with confidence or immobilize you with fear. Creating anything in this life doesn't happen without input, organization, and computation from the mind. Even when we are knocking on death's door, the mind has a say.

Incredible loss such as yours and mine activates the mind with deep questions concerning life and its purpose. Perhaps you've had these thoughts swirling in the back (or the front) of your mind for some time.

▶ Why MY son? Why MY daughter?
▶ Why did this happen to me? I'm a good person! A good parent!
▶ What am I supposed to do with my life now? I have no hope.
▶ What's the point of life?
▶ What really happens when you die?
▶ Where was God?

Grief can keep you tethered to the shadows of the mind. These questions can either ensnare you in self-pity or they can trigger a desire for answers. Seeking answers initiates movement. And just the tiniest bit of movement will loosen the chains of grief that bind you and set you on a path to a joyful and meaningful life. When you embark on this path you move toward the light. The light of your soul that is calling you to a life of joy!

When you indulge in a search for an explanation to the deep questions mentioned above, allow yourself to be open to *any* possibility. The answers may show up in the most unexpected moments and from the unlikeliest of sources. Seek, my friend. Seek until you find answers that you can live with. Answers that set you free from the bondage of grief and allow you to live with your sadness from a place of grace and deep self-respect.

CONFRONTING THE SELF-PITY OF SORROW

Many people, in the wake of a tragic loss, give up. They take on the mantle of grief – and its accessorizing partner, self-pity – and they surrender hope. The worrisome rhetoric of the mind takes over and becomes the new normal. Perhaps this has happened to you or someone you love. Maybe you have convinced yourself that you don't have a choice. But you do. Where your life was once a brilliant cerulean blue, it now could be a rich midnight blue. The color, texture, and tone of your life has certainly changed, and you get to decide who you are in relationship to that new normal. You can be vibrantly alive, purposeful, and blessed even now.

You must be willing to release the negative mental

churning. To live a gratifying life you have to change your mind. Changing your mind does not mean resisting the deep questions. It doesn't mean ignoring sadness and pain. Reclaiming your joy means you embrace ALL of your life experiences, all of your thoughts, all of your feelings. You begin to seek solutions and new ways of living, of being in relationship, of loving and of serving. You pursue peace of mind. You listen to your emotional heart. You explore pleasure. Doing nothing, allowing the mind frantic free reign, will create a downward spiral into abysmal depression and self-pity. This will shackle you in the victim mindset and you will not feel good about yourself, your life, or the people around you.

The victim state keeps you small and powerless. When you surrender to that, you give the people around you the message that it's ok, even a welcomed response, for them to feel sorry for you. When others feel sorry for you, when you feel sorry for yourself, for an extended period of time, the unspoken messages become:

▶ You poor thing
▶ You are helpless
▶ You have no power
▶ There is no hope

I have never wanted people to *feel sorry for me.* If anything I prefer for people to *feel sad with me.* When someone is willing to step into the ring of sadness with me and cry with me for a bit or maybe hug me, I tend to be able to turn it around much more quickly. Inevitably, within a few minutes I'm able to find a smile and a giggle. Before too long we both are in a much better place.

Grief shared is half the sorrow. Happiness shared is twice the joy.
— Swedish Proverb

I have a lovely friend who I've known for over thirty years. We taught school together, bought houses in the same neighborhood, had babies at the same time, and went camping together. When Aleisha passed away, my friend would come over every day and would just sit and cry with me. We'd reminisce about silly antics the kids exhibited when they were younger. We'd giggle through our tears and disbelief. In the years following the accident, there were many, many times when I would be out shopping and would hear a song that would send me into a tearful state. I always called Paula. I never got the sense that Paula felt sorry for me. Maybe she did, but she never said that to me or treated me that way. She always, no matter where she was, willingly stepped into the ring of sorrow with me. She would listen to me express my sadness of the moment and she would cry with me. And without fail, we would always end in a fit of giggles through the remembering. As fate would have it, nine years after Aleisha transitioned to heaven, Paula's son also made his heavenly transition via suicide. Now we truly share in the sorrow and in the joy of each other, of our kids, of ourselves.

To find your way to a life of joy you must be willing to lay down depression and self-pity. Dwelling in the dark circle of self-pity and depression is inevitable as a grieving mother, for a time. It's natural and gives attention to the turbulent emotions of grief. But there must be a time limit, a point where you consciously choose to pull yourself up from that well of darkness and reach toward the light again. It takes courage and determination to step out of that circle.

The shadow side of your mind plays tricks on you and makes you think that if you turn your back on the victim mentality and turn your face toward the sun, you will forget your child and you will accept that they are gone.

Nothing could be further from the truth. You *know* that you will never forget your child. They are a part of you. Their energy lives on in you via your beautiful memories with them. Your memories are the light aspects of your mind. It is the positive memories of your time with your loved one that keeps the love alive between the two of you even though they are in heaven.

Continually holding yourself in the place of the victim, no matter the trauma or tragedy, keeps you in pain. This is a choice you are making. Yes, others may contribute with comments like, "Poor you" or "I feel sorry for you." These comments validate the image you continue to hold of yourself as the victim. Being the victim gets you attention. It gets you hugs, discounts, free stuff. But the victim mentality also keeps you small and invisible and ir-*response*-able for your life.

THIS is NOT the intention of your soul. Your soul longs for you to step into your life fully, embracing the good, the bad, the happy, the sad. I repeat: the good, bad, happy, and sad are parts that make up the wholeness of you. Those qualities exist in your life today. It is your birthright as a human being to experience all of those qualities...... the wholeness of you. YOU are the one withholding them from your life experience, and grief is your excuse.

You can turn your face to the radiance of joy and fulfillment. All you have to do is change your mind.

Retraining the mind requires willingness first and foremost. You must have a desire to get out of the victim mentality. Focusing your attention on when, where, and with whom you easily slip into self-pity mode is also important. In addition, owning your shadow side and its inherent imperfection is a vital component in moving away from grief and toward joy. We're human. We make mistakes. Just because we're grieving doesn't mean we've suddenly become angelic. In fact, I have seen numerous women who are deep in grief become raging bitches – as if grief is a license to become a bitch. Not on the path to joy! When you're sad, mad, worried, frustrated, afraid, and then you mess up? ADMIT IT! Admission swiftly and cleanly resets your mind and your heart, and healing is almost instantaneous. You literally feel the release of agitated energy!

Consider these questions:

▶ How long have you been grieving?
▶ Are you mired in self-pity?
▶ How is the victim mentality benefitting you?
▶ Who is suffering by you staying in the circle of self-pity?
▶ Do you like yourself as the victim?
▶ Is this really how you want to live out the remaining days of your life?

Who makes the sun light up my shadow when the darkness tries to follow me?
— Jaci Velasquez, You

FREEDOM FROM VICTIM MANTRA

The word *mantra* means an incantation or prayer; a sacred word or symbol used as an object of concentration. Mantras have been used for millennia in meditation and to help re-pattern the mind. I have personally used and taught mantras for years. For me the mantra becomes a personal hymn of transformation. You can use any mantra to assist in changing your mind. Make sure your mantra is a positive, forward-looking statement of change. Here is one to use until you create your own. Feel free to tweak this to accommodate your situation.

> I see the beauty all around me and I allow it to open my heart and change my mind. Life is glorious!

COMING FACE TO FACE WITH MY OWN SELF-PITY

One day, about 18-24 months after Aleisha passed away, I spent an afternoon with a friend of mine who has studied with some contemporary spiritual masters. My friend had heard the story of Aleisha's accident and transition to heaven. That afternoon I was again sharing pieces of my story with him. When I paused, he asked, "How many times a week do you share this story?" I said I didn't know. What he said next initially offended me. But as I reflected on it, I realized his words were true. He said, "Every time you share your story you perpetuate your own pain. You keep yourself stuck in grief."

Ouch! "But my grief is REAL," my mind shouted. "And YOU haven't lost your daughter. You have NO idea what I'm going through, how much my life has changed." My friend was not intending to step on my toes. He spoke with tremendous love. This was a pivotal moment for me. As I reflected on his statement over the next several weeks, I released my hurt feelings and examined his words. Slowly I began to see that this was a message from my soul, and likely from Aleisha. It began to feel like an invitation to adopt a new way of life that contained grief, but didn't dwell there. Since that time I have refined the way I tell my story. Today I am able to deliver my story without triggering an emotional meltdown. You see, I don't want to ruin anyone's day with my sad story. That story is mine. I live with it moment to moment. At the same time, I can't not talk about Aleisha. So I have found a way to share her story with as much light and joy as I can verbally craft.

Dramatically sharing your story on a regular basis is keeping you depressed. It's keeping you in pain. It's blocking your path to a fulfilling life within a new normal. It's keeping you from reclaiming joy. Undoubtedly your story has become more dramatic with the telling. Mine did. That's human nature.

Susan was a client who was two and half years into her grief journey. She longed to find a life of fulfillment again after her twenty-two-year-old daughter passed away from ovarian cancer. She practiced yoga, attended church, and read books, but she just couldn't seem to move out from under the burden of grief. She had established a beautiful practice of honoring her daughter with both family and personal ritual. She wanted to live her life in honor of her daughter's courageous fight but was immobilized by the heaviness and darkness of her grief.

In a coaching session, she was sharing details of a recent vacation she had been on with her husband. She off-handedly mentioned sharing the story of her beloved daughter's passing with everyone she met on her trip. As I listened to her I realized she really did mean EVERYONE! People in the stores where she shopped. Couples she ran into at a bar. The resort staff, and so on. As much as Susan wanted to move into a life of joy, she was keeping herself mired in sorrow by her endless storytelling.

I invited her to do an experiment for two weeks and scale down her storytelling to about two minutes. At the end of two weeks, Susan noticed that she felt less anxiety. After she was comfortable with that storytelling style, I encouraged her to pare down her story even more and to make it as neutral as possible while still honoring her daughter. I eventually asked her to create a thirty-second story that she could relate with neutral emotion. It took some practice. Susan found she got very specific about the words she chose to share. She moved into a more mindful storytelling, which ultimately liberated her from anxiety and mental churning, and even helped relieve some tension in her body. She continues her practice of mindful storytelling to this day.

TIP #3: REFRAME YOUR STORYTELLING

1. What are you getting from sharing your story?
2. How does making it more dramatic serve you?
3. What would happen if you stopped telling your story, stopped identifying yourself as a grieving mother?
4. What are you afraid of if you decrease your storytelling?
5. How can you make your story a one-line statement or a 30-second statement?

Telling your story over and over again, adding dramatic detail, generally draws pity from another. That feeds you in some way and it keeps you in a cycle of victim mentality. Some people get so stuck here that they become a self-fulfilling prophecy, creating a delicious, (or vicious) cycle of dramatic storytelling, anchoring in pain, and extending the victim mentality.

Brenda and Julie were two women who came to me for yoga within a few weeks of each other. Each of them had lost young adult children. Julie had numbed out, had stopped eating and was participating minimally in life. Her family was quite concerned about her. She told the story of her journey into grief in a brief, rapid statement. I got the impression she just wanted to get through it. Brenda was participating in life, barely. Even though it had been three years since the accident, the way she told her story of her grief I thought the accident had occurred within the last year.

I worked with these women for several months using both yoga and coaching techniques. Julie responded immediately. Each time she stepped onto her mat and moved her body, I could see more serenity in her countenance. Within just a few months of coaching and yoga, she became reacquainted with her zest for life. The true catalyst for her vital regeneration came through some particularly exquisite food that was served at a retreat. It was savoring the aromas and flavors of the food that moved her out of her bland existence of grief and into a delectable experience of the pleasures of life. Julie was ready and willing to change the way she had been thinking and living, to come out of the dark hollows of her grief. She immediately started to participate in life again.

Brenda took a bit more time. It felt like she was cemented in her grief, her self-pity, and her focus on what the rest of her family wasn't doing to serve her, understand her, and make her happy. Her journey to reclaiming a life of joy took a bit longer and required her to do some deep soul-searching into how she was perpetuating her stuck state via her own pity party. She did eventually take responsibility and find her path to a joyful life.

Returning to joy hasn't meant that these beautiful souls have forgotten their kids. They have precious memories and rituals that keep them connected to the past and their loved ones, but they are free. Free to live a life of joy.

Free–can you imagine what it would feel like to be free from the incredible heaviness of grief? Setting yourself free is a gift you give yourself – and it can be done using simple techniques that gently guide you toward joy, and honor the beautiful soul of your heavenly child.

TELL YOUR STORY WITH INTEGRITY

For the next two weeks, I invite you to begin to refine your story of grief. You can experiment with the actual words you use. By the end of two weeks, try to have shortened your story down to no more than a minute or two. The goal is to leave you feeling content in the honoring of your child and inspired by your courage. I want you to begin to be quietly inspired by your life. You are brave, beautiful, and needed. Once you've mastered the two-minute story, whittle it down to thirty seconds. After lots of practice, when you meet someone new and they ask how many children you have, make a simple, factual statement. Take notice of how you feel, and pay attention to the facial expressions and response of others. Remember that we're practicing ways of establishing a new normal for you that allows you to honor your departed loved and honor your continuing life on the planet. Remain in your vital integrity as you consciously change your mind toward a new way of living.

Integrity
[in-*teg*-ri-tee]
noun
2. the state of being whole, entire, or undiminished
(Dictionary.com)

CHAPTER 4

Gentle Movement
Releases Tension

Our practice takes us into the unknown. We deliberately head out into new terrain, off the charts of our familiar world. Such exploration calls for radical faith.... We will have bad days and good days, in practice as in life. Sometimes the progress of yesterday seems to have evaporated today. And yet there is always movement. As long as we show up and do the work, healing will happen. — *Rolf Gates*, Meditations from the Mat

PEOPLE OFTEN ASK ME, "HOW did you do it?" My answer always includes this statement, "Yoga saved me!" A lovely neighbor of mine was teaching yoga in her home, and I had started a regular practice just one month before Aleisha passed away. After the accident, yoga became my solitary grieving time. I could feel my community observing me and my boys as we navigated the early stages of grief. Many times I was comforting and uplifting students, parents, friends, and family, doing my best to let them know how much they meant to Aleisha. While I cried with many of these lovely people, I didn't have a lot of alone time initially to be in my own grief. Yoga provided that for me. As I moved my body, I was literally moving the intense emotion of grief through and out of my body. Sometimes I would just lie on my mat and sob. My yoga teacher (and the others in the class) were incredibly gracious to hold the space for that healing practice. As the years progressed, spending time on my mat became a reliable resource for processing any kind of intense stress and emotion. The combination of movement with focused breathing soothed me on many levels. It was so impactful that I eventually got certified to teach yoga.

THE EFFECTS OF STRESS AND TRAUMA ON THE BODY

It is fairly common in our society for people to store the stress of their careers in their neck and shoulders. The demands of our fast-paced lives combined with our high-tech culture of cell phones, tablets, and laptop computers all contribute to hunched shoulders and the neck sticking out in front the body. That translates into a stiff neck and tight shoulders.

You have experienced the devouring nature of the intense emotions contained in grief. Chances are that you haven't processed all of this energy because it's just too much; truly, you must process it in layers. The initial impact of these intense feelings is likely still contained within your body.

There are hundreds of articles explaining how the body stores the energy of emotion in your skin, your organs, your muscles and joints, even your cells. It's interesting to note that often we verbally describe this held tension. For instance, excess energy stored in the shoulders becomes an extra "burden" that we "shoulder" and that leads to a "pain in the neck." We also store excess emotional tension in the hips, and we often say, "This is such a pain in the butt!" Stiffness is defined as inflexibility. Have you ever referred to yourself or someone else as being flexible or inflexible? This can be an unconscious statement of truth about both our bodies and our capacity to show up in a relationship.

You've undoubtedly heard of post-traumatic stress disorder (PTSD). Most of us associate that with people who have served in the military. But I know from my own experience, and that of numerous clients, that the death of a loved one is a significant and overwhelming trauma. The American Heritage Stedman's Medical Dictionary defines PTSD as: *An anxiety disorder affecting individuals who have experienced profound emotional trauma, such as torture, rape, military combat, or a natural disaster, characterized by recurrent flashbacks of the traumatic event, nightmares, eating disorders, anxiety, fatigue, forgetfulness, and social withdrawal.*

As I've already mentioned, grief can become an all-consuming and disorienting force in your life. It's nearly impossible to deal with all of that overwhelming emotion at once. You know that you process it in layers, dealing with bits and pieces as you are able, just as a military veteran processes PTSD.

SENSATIONAL SHACKLES

I bet you can still quite easily go back to the moment you received the news that your child had died. Perhaps there was a heaviness in your gut and/or your heart. Maybe your heart was racing. Perhaps you felt shaky all over and nauseous. Martha Beck calls this "shackles on" in her book *Steering by Starlight*. The "shackles test" tells you *where* your body stores an emotional response to a situation. You can use this simple tool with a variety of events in your life, both positive and negative. Like the P/P Scale, simply recall a negative, emotionally charged moment in your life and notice the physical sensations you experience. Then remember a moment that was uplifting and joyful and attune to what your body experiences. "Shackles on" experiences tend to activate the fight, flight, or flee response of the sympathetic nervous system: literally hair-raising (back of the neck, arms), heart racing, lump in your throat, weight in your stomach and more!

When trauma occurs, our sympathetic nervous system goes into overdrive to protect us or help us deal with the trauma. But trauma, by its very nature, is overwhelming, and more often than not we aren't prepared in the moment of trauma (and for many moments beyond the initial event) to deal with so much all-consuming energy. So the body becomes a self-storage unit for all that excess energy.

The symptoms of this storage overload include tightness in the neck and shoulders (*pain in the neck or frozen shoulder*), migraines (*can't wrap my head around this*), low-back pain (*threw my back out*), hip tightness and discomfort (*pain in the butt*), digestive and elimination issues (*I'm having a hard time digesting this*), circulatory issues, and much more. We unconsciously speak the truth of what is going on physiologically between the thoughts, the emotions and the body.

TIP #4: USE GENTLE YOGA TO RELIEVE TENSION IN THE BODY

Yoga has become a household word in our culture. But it is often misunderstood. Many people believe that in order to practice yoga you have to be a human pretzel, raising your leg over your head and resting it on the back of your neck. I'm sure you've been standing in line at your natural food store and seen the one of the many yoga magazines with svelte, beautiful women on the cover doing incredible bends, twists, etc. I can tell you, as a seasoned yoga instructor, that those abilities are not the norm. There are millions of yoga students and teachers who are not human pretzels. Yoga really can be accessible to anyone, from the able-bodied and in-shape to those who are wheelchair-bound.

Yoga, and its corresponding breath work (pranayama), are gentle ways to begin to relieve tension in the body. The word yoga means to unite. The practice of moving with focused breathing literally slows the heartbeat as well as racing thoughts. Yoga lowers the blood pressure and calms anxious feelings. It increases strength and flexibility and brings a renewal to the body. The alignment of breath and movement can elicit healing of the entire being: body, mind, emotions, spirit.

We will explore a more focused yoga sequence in the next chapter. For now, I'll go over three exercises that help establish a foundational awareness of what is going on in your body in the present moment.

Yoga has many aspects beyond the physical (*asana*) practice. In fact, there are eight limbs, or aspects, of yoga. Each of these in their own right can have a healing effect on the practitioner.

- ▶ Yoga poses *(asana)*
- ▶ Breath work (*pranayama*)
- ▶ Inner reflection (*pratyhara*)
- ▶ Focused mind (*dharna*)

▶ Meditation (*dhyana*)
▶ Connecting with Divine consciousness (*samadhi*)

The remaining two limbs of yoga are the *yamas* and *niyamas*. These are external and internal guidelines for "right living." Most often, in this country, we practice only one limb of the eight-limbed path of yoga – the physical practice. This is a great place to start, as it is through the physical practice of yoga that we begin to cultivate awareness of the more subtle energies of our body, our mind, our devotion, and the purpose of our life... but more on that later.

Physical yoga practice, in one sense, is a merging awareness of life and death. Of movement and stillness. At the beginning of class, we engage in focused breathing and gentle movement, sometimes ramping up to vibrant *vinyasa* flow. Our heart rate may elevate; we may sweat as we feel the pulse of life (*prana*) moving through us. All of this activity leads us, at the end of the class, to *savasana*, which literally translates as "corpse pose." What better way to help us *move* the stagnant energy of grief through our bodies? Yoga has the power to transform our bodies, retrain our minds, soothe our emotions, and renew our spirits.

The physical (*asana*) practice of yoga has done wonders for hundreds of thousands of people by helping to relieve tightness, release stored-up emotion, and clarify conflicting thoughts. As mentioned previously, most of us hold tension in our neck and shoulders. This leads to migraines, frozen shoulders, and rotator cuff issues. The lower back is another point in the body where people experience a concentration of stress, perhaps from collapsing on the lumbar spine. Tightness in the hips is quite common due to our sedentary lifestyles and sitting at desks for many hours a day, year after year. Now compound the tightness in those areas with the stress, the heaviness, and the emotional burden of grief, and you can see why people often develop unusual medical conditions after the loss of a loved one.

I've developed a gentle yoga flow that anyone can do. Yep! Anyone. Don't worry if you don't think you can get down, or back up, from the floor. This is a chair yoga sequence, and it's a great place to start if you're new to yoga or need a refreshing, gentle flow. This is a variation of a sequence I teach in almost every yoga class. It's a lovely, simple beginning practice that helps you learn to listen to the messages of your body and release the tension of stored emotion. Making the simple decision that you are ready to let go of some of the long-stored energy offers the first layer of relief. As you practice this sequence daily, you will likely notice greater relief. To experience the full class visit www. griefinterruptedbook.com

Here is a brief excerpt from the class:

Exercise 1: Seated Alignment and Full Breath

Using your P/P Scale, check in with your body right now and see how it is feeling as you sit in your chair. Without making any adjustments, feel your butt and thighs sitting on the chair. Become aware of your spine resting against the back of the chair. Take notice of where your shoulders are in relation to your hips. Are they rounding forward or rolling back? Is your chest caving in, or is it erect, almost reaching forward? Pay particular attention to your spine. Does it feel lengthened or collapsed? Where is your chin?

Is it sticking out in front of your shoulders or is it floating naturally at the top of your spine?

Surrendering to a rounded spine, hunched shoulders, and extended chin, try to take a deep inhale and a complete exhale. It's nearly impossible. Next bring your shoulders into alignment over your hips with your ears lined up over your shoulders. Extend the top (crown) of your head toward the ceiling. Notice how much taller you feel. Now take a slow, deep inhale, followed by a leisurely, complete exhale. Repeat several times. In this posture you are giving yourself a *full* breathing experience.

Simply becoming more mindful of how you sit, stand, and breathe will start to have a magical effect on how you live each moment of your life. You will be infusing your body with more oxygen, which will elevate your mood and motivation. With an elevated mood, you naturally create space for hope to move into your being. Hope is the precursor to joy.

After several breaths from seated alignment, notice how your body feels. Is your mind clearer? Perhaps your emotions feel calm. Return to the P/P Scale for a follow-up assessment.

Exercise 2: Life Force Reach

This is a simple exercise I learned from my dear friend Sherry Zak Morris of Yoga Vista Academy. When I perform this stretch daily, I always imagine that I am reaching out and grabbing as much of life's pleasure and delight as I possibly can hold. Life force, or *prana*, is the Sanskrit word for "energy of life." It's that esoteric pulse that makes trees grow, allows birds to soar, and motivates bees to search for flower nectar. Life force, prana, infuses us with desire to live our life according to our own uniqueness – our own soul plan. The despair of mourning is a slow, sluggish form of life force, and it's "sticky," which often leads us to become enmeshed in the hollows of sadness. We must thoughtfully choose to raise ourselves up with a more vibrant pulse of life force.

Come to seated alignment with shoulders over hips, spine lengthened, and your ears lined up over your shoulders. Keep your chin parallel with the floor. Extend your arms out to each side, with your arms parallel to the floor. Take several deep, slow, full rounds of breath. With each round of breath imagine extending your arms another inch allowing you to reach out and touch more and more life force with every breathing cycle. You will notice a lovely stretching sensation moving from your shoulders all the way down your arms and into your hands and fingers. You may even notice that stretching sensation originates in your neck. Take five complete rounds of breath, savoring the sensations. Then release your arms down and shake them out. Wrap yourself up in a hug.

I have a beautiful yoga student named Sandy who is a schoolteacher. She attends as many yoga classes as she can fit in each week to help balance the energies of her students as well as the demands and expectations of the school system administration. Sandy will show up week to week with various new tight spots. She quickly shares what body parts are speaking to her and then she settles into the space of her mat. When she closes her eyes, I can almost feel the power of her intention to create a sacred space around her mat. She'll move through the class with us, often laughing along with our silly antics. While she acknowledges the energy of the group, she is always a bit detached and very obviously focused on the internal experience of her practice.

When we reach the final pose, *savasana*, she surrenders to the stillness of that moment, however long (or short) it happens to last. As she arises from *savasana*, I have noticed that without exception, there is a look of bliss on her face. Her eyes are closed, she's smiling, and she's owning the gift of restoration that she just gave herself. It's a beautiful thing to witness each week. In addition to her present-life demands, Sandy is a breast cancer survivor. The value that she places on each moment, on every breath, on each movement is ever-evident on her face.

When the body is relaxed and in its natural state, it can respond to the "good stress" of deep concentrated breathing, resistance training, and movement. Thus, gentle yoga, guided meditation, and breath work are the best ways to begin to unite your body, mind, and emotions with healing. When you begin to heal physically, you move into a state of greater well-being, which is fertile ground for the germination of sustained joy.

You are ready to try yoga for yourself. Your first class may not be as blissful as Sandy's experience, above. But keep at it. Listen to what your body is telling you as you move and breathe. If you experience excruciating pain, come out of the pose gently. You will experience stretching and a bit of discomfort initially. That's normal and means that you are likely bringing great benefit to your body. Take a moment right now and assess where you are feeling tightness, discomfort, pain. Then indulge in a few long, slow inhales and exhales.

Now you're ready! Enjoy your practice!

Visit www.griefinterruptedbook.com for the complete class and other tools to help you reclaim your joy.

You must learn to be still in the midst of activity and to be vibrantly alive in repose.— Indira Ghandi

CHAPTER 5

Just Breathe – Again!

The practice of moment to moment, nonjudgmental awareness brings focus to
whatever is happening in the moment, and it is only in the present
moment that you can make changes.
– *Bob Stahl, Elisha Goldstein*, Mindfulness Based Stress Reduction Workbook

THE INTENSE ENERGY FROM THE swirling thoughts
and emotions of grief is often too much to process in
a short period of time. So our wise bodies store that
unexpressed energy until we're ready to look at it, deal
with it, and release it. In this chapter, we will dive deeper
into the release of stored energy in the physical body
through the breath and movement. Before we take that
journey, pause for a moment of profound gratitude for
your body. Place one hand on your heart and one hand
on your belly. Now take a long, slow inhale and feel
the intercostal muscles (the muscles between your ribs)
expand. Pause ever so briefly at the top of your inhale
and savor the fullness of your lungs. Then indulge in a
slow, complete exhale, noticing the brief moment before
you take another inhale. Repeat this three times and
then just let yourself relax and breathe normally. Tell
your body thank you for continuing to serve you.

It may seem elemental to practice breathing consciously and to coordinate movement with the rhythm of the breath. Rolf Gates, author of *Meditations from the Mat* says about yoga practice: that "... we seek answers outside ourselves, when in fact the answers lie within. We look out into the material world and identify ourselves with it. Identified with the material world that is completely beyond our control, we are consumed with fear. This fear is at the root of all of our afflictions.... The good news is that yoga systematically deconstructs this fear... Yoga is a path to our true nature. This truth can be easily tested at the conclusion of every *asana* (yoga pose) practice."

He goes on to mention that many yoga students experience a sort of "coming home" in the quietude of *savasana*, the final pose of the class. This is a coming home to the self, the body, the life, the spirit. "The coming home is real," Rolf says. "You have come closer to the truth about yourself, and that is why you feel peace."

Consider the following story of one of my students, Vikki, whose awakening to her long-held breathing patterns was inspirational. Vikki was a beautiful middle-aged woman who attended my evening yoga classes after she got off work. She was dedicated and focused in her practice. I noticed that during our breathing exercises at the beginning of class, she would scrunch up her face in what looked like excruciating pain. When I asked her about this, she waved her hand and said dismissively, "Oh, it just hurts when I breathe." When I asked her where it hurt, she said, "Everywhere!" I encouraged her to back off a bit and not breathe quite as deep in order to alleviate the pain.

One day she had the day off work and attended my morning yoga class. This time when we engaged in focused breathing at the beginning of class, her face was relaxed, almost blissful. I asked her about her experience and she said, "It felt SO GOOD to breathe deeply! And it didn't hurt at all. I realized this morning that I don't breathe when I'm at work." She reflected that she was incredibly tense at work, with her shoulders rounding forward and her spine curved. This posture was one she had maintained for eight or more hours per day for years. There was literally no room for her lungs to expand and for her intercostal muscles (the muscles between the ribs) to flex and contract. These muscles were weak, tight, and out of shape. This was an incredibly valuable awakening for Vikki. After this dawning, she began a regular practice of deep breathing in the morning to start her day. She had sticky note reminders in her car and on her computer screen to help retrain herself toward better physical alignment and deeper breathing cycles.

The point here is that the simple act of deep breathing did not feel good to her, in the beginning, due to the incredible stress that her body was storing. Luckily, she was open to listening to the messages of her body and was committed to taking steps to support her body and release the stress as much as she was able to.

Many of us are walking, standing, or sitting in a manner that promotes shallow breath and constricts the flow of life force energy, not to mention causing stunted oxygen intake and restricted carbon dioxide release. We are literally sabotaging our lives with every breath. The refreshing healing in-flow of oxygen is reduced, leaving us feeling tired, depressed, unmotivated. The out breath is rarely complete, leaving toxic energy in our system.

LEARNING TO BREATHE – AGAIN!

I heard once that we learn how to breathe from our primary caregiver. Recall your childhood caregiver. Consider the demands and stresses of their life back in the day. I'm sure you can imagine their lack of awareness about how they were breathing. For the most part this was not something people cared about unless they were ill. This disconnection from the most basic life function is how *you* learned to breathe and how you likely learned to ignore your body. It's time we learned to breathe – again!

At this point you have an awareness and experience of breathing deeply and deliciously. Just shifting your attention to lengthening each inhale and completing each exhale will initiate a renewal of life force throughout your being. In addition, all the systems of your physical body will operate with greater efficiency. Your mind will become clearer and anxiety will gradually dissipate. These are the benefits from simply breathing a full and complete cycle.

In addition to learning shallow breathing from our caregivers, we also learned at a young age to discredit our emotions. The emotions are like our internal barometer. They reveal the truth about how we feel. This automatic barometer reading often is not considered trustworthy. So, to make us feel better, our thoughts begin to do "damage control" and dramatic storytelling; blaming others and avoiding taking responsibility become our coping strategies. Over the course of our lives, the unexpressed energy of our thoughts and feelings gets stored in our bodies as tension, fatigue, fat, and dis-ease. This is an unconscious, ongoing pattern in most of us. We will explore the emotions deeper in later chapters. It's important to note here that suppressed emotions and shallow breathing go hand in hand.

Add to these classic patterns a major trauma like the death of your daughter or son, or any significant loss that overwhelms your system, and you have just compounded the stress factor in your body significantly. With reduced oxygen to your blood and organs and an appreciable increase to your cortisol levels (the stress hormone) your body is likely FREAKING OUT!

TIP #5: BREATHE TO RELIEVE

No matter where you are or what you are doing, you can alter the way you breathe within the space of moment and experience a level of stress and tension relief. A simple change in your breathing technique can bring stress recovery, clarity, stability, wisdom, and more, depending on your need and the situation at hand.

Typically when you read about the breath, you also learn about the sympathetic and parasympathetic nervous system and how they are associated with the breath. Sometimes the descriptions can be long and overly scientific. Dr. Al Sears, an anti-aging pioneer, wrote the following simple explanation in his blog post, *Breathe a Sigh of Relief*:

> When you breathe in, it's sympathetic – fight or flight. One example would be gasping in shock.
>
> When you breathe out, that's para-sympathetic – relaxing.
>
> Again, it's in our language. For example, "breathe a sigh of relief" or "waiting to exhale."

You are probably already using your breath as a way to relieve stress and to calm yourself. It is a natural response for us to sigh when we're stressed, worried, anxious, or confused. Some specialists believe that sighing is a way to reset the balance between the sympathetic and parasympathetic nervous systems.

BREATHING THE ELEMENTS

In my journey of recovery from grief, I repeatedly stumbled across teachers of breath work, meditation, and chanting who used the four elements – Earth, Air, Fire, and Water – to teach their methodology. Utilizing the energy from these four elements was natural for me. It reconnected me to nature, and had the effect of returning me to my innate wisdom. I believe this return to the calm within helped accelerate my healing process. These practices arrived in my life from various belief systems – Celtic wisdom, Sufism, Christianity and yoga, to name a few.

A book that had a particularly strong impact on me was *Living from the Heart* by Puran and Susanna Bair. Puran and Susanna teach a variety of breathing techniques along with their Heart Rhythm Meditation to bring forth energy, clarity, peace, joy, and inner power.

In *Living from the Heart*, the Bairs state that though the elements are not recognized by the scientific community in a favorable manner, culturally they are valuable to us as a way to sort out the some of the confusing inner experiences we have.

"We have fire experiences that rise up and lift our emotions, leading to exaltation. Water experiences flow downward and lead to grace and acceptance. Earth experiences that spread out horizontally and give us stability and control. Air experiences of the mind independent of direction that give us awareness of the hearts of others."

To experience these benefits of the four elements through the breath, the Bairs suggests four different breathing techniques:

ELEMENT	BREATHE IN	BREATHE OUT
AIR	Mouth	Mouth
FIRE	Mouth	Nose
WATER	Nose	Mouth
EARTH	Nose	Nose

As I began to practice these breathing patterns, I realized that I often will resort naturally to these various patterns depending on the life circumstance. I'm sure you do, too, if you stop to notice. For instance, when I'm seeking clarity or trying to remember something I will often move into the air breath. The air breath (mouth/mouth) often initiates a much-needed shift in my perspective. If I'm in need of an emotional release, I will naturally move into the water breath (nose/mouth). A deep, nurturing inhale, followed by a potent and full exhale always soothes my emotional state. When I need to relax, as I do when trying to go to sleep, I assume the Earth breathing pattern (nose/nose). The slow, rhythmic inhalation and exhalation through the nose reminds me of the rhythm of the ocean waves and calms my entire system. Fire breath (mouth/nose) was the most challenging for me to practice. It didn't feel natural until I realized that when I'm frustrated or mad, I "release fire" energy naturally through the fire breath by taking a deep inhale through the mouth and sharp exhale through the nose. Sort of like a fire-breathing dragon! As I worked with these breathing patterns consciously, their effectiveness increased. I'm certain they will for you as well.

Take a few minutes right now to play with these various techniques. Notice which ones are easy and which ones are more difficult. Is there one that makes you feel uplifted? How about calming? Do any of them make you feel anxious? Try not to judge any of the techniques as being good or bad. Just notice your response to them.

To learn more about the heart rhythm method and breathing the elements, visit www.iamheart.org.

RELIEF THROUGH BREATH

Joanne wanted to give yoga a try. She was middle-aged, out of shape, and, unknown to me, grieving the loss of her son two years prior. Joanne was a lovely woman with soft blonde hair, gentle facial features, and captivating green eyes. My first impression of her was that her spirit and her *prana* (life force) were being overshadowed by the stresses of life. She looked exhausted, with dark circles under her eyes. She never smiled, and her words were clipped and lacked expression. She "felt" heavy-laden with what I sensed was some form of unexpressed emotion.

The theme I had chosen for that particular class was "connect to your wholeness." I shared simple deep breathing techniques along with gentle movement sequences. As the class progressed, I observed a startling transformation in Joanne. Within the first five minutes, simply seated, quiet and calm, she started crying. The tears continued throughout the class. As I am wont to do, I infused the class with moments of humor, always returning back to the notion, "You Are Whole, just as you are." I noticed at one point she allowed a brief grin to emerge in the midst of her tears.

At the end of class, the tears momentarily subsided as Joanne approached me. The most notable thing about her was the radiant smile on her face. She had literally transformed in sixty minutes. I was startled by her incredible beauty! I hugged her and said, "Welcome to yoga! We've all been there in a puddle on our mats. Yoga is like that!"

She smiled and began to share her story of grief and loss. Naturally, we bonded instantly. As I got to know Joanne over the course of several months I came to recognize that familiar pattern of "all work and no play." In other words, Joanne was totally out of touch with what brought her pleasure in life. She worked hard at her job and when she had some quiet time, she disappeared into her grief. As she committed to a regular yoga practice, I started to notice that when she arrived to class she would flash a smile so radiant, she lit up the room. When I pointed that out to her, she balked, but slowly she allowed that radiance to shine a little bit longer each week. Motivated by her growth, I established class themes that focused on experiencing the pleasures of life. It became clear to me that the more she experienced the pleasure of moving her body and connecting with her breath, the more she smiled. It was a subtle shift that happened over several months and Joanne didn't give herself credit for it immediately. With encouragement, she began to own the shift toward joy. She told me one day, with great satisfaction, that her family had noticed the change in her and that they had told her how happy that made them.

CHAPTER 6

Take a Sojourn

Before embarking on important undertakings, sit quietly, calm your senses and thoughts, and meditate deeply. You will then be guided by the great creative power of Spirit. After that you should utilize all necessary material means to achieve your goal. – Parmahansa Yogananda

AROUND THE ONE-YEAR ANNIVERSARY OF Aleisha's accident, I took myself on a sojourn to a little town in Colorado called Crestone. There is NOTHING in Crestone except two ashrams and two stupas, two – maybe three now – Buddhist centers, a Carmelite Monastery, Native American sacred sites, hot springs, and more in the realm of spiritual retreat centers. What there isn't, is shopping or dining (a restaurant or two – no more). There are mountain vistas that will truly take your breath away. The energy is *so* pure in Crestone, I always say even the high desert shrubs glow. It is *so* quiet in Crestone you can hear yourself breathing softly. Crestone is truly a vortex of spiritual energy. It is about a three-and-a-half hour drive from Denver through the majestic Rocky Mountains. Each mile takes you deeper into yourself, if you pay attention to it.

I booked myself at a bed and breakfast (aka a spare room in a woman's house). I arrived after dark and met the woman in her kitchen. We chatted a bit and as I prepared to go to my room I noticed she had Angel Cards on her counter. Angel Cards are tiny cards with one word on them. The idea is that you will draw the card with the word you most need to meditate on. That first night, I picked TRUTH.

The next morning I awoke to a lovely breakfast waiting on the kitchen table for me. The proprietor had left for her day job in the nearest town – fifty miles away! As I was leaving the kitchen to get ready for my "big day of exploration," I passed by the bowl of Angel Cards and, after shuffling them a bit, picked TRUTH. Naturally, I giggled a little.

I visited one of the ashrams that day because I had never been to one and I was curious. I went into the beautiful meditation temple, took off my shoes, and walked around the warm, empty room, marveling at the array of fresh flowers they had strewn around their goddess statue. When I say "warm room," I mean like the warmest, safest hug you've ever had. It was cold and windy that autumn day, and the temple was quiet, peaceful, and warm. I sat quietly for some time, allowing myself to simply soften a bit.

Later that day I returned to the B&B and, just for additional giggles, I shuffled the Angel cards and drew one – TRUTH! This time I laughed out loud!

The second morning I had exactly the same experience and drew... you guessed it... TRUTH!

I didn't draw a card that evening. On my third and last morning in Crestone, the proprietor was home and I shared with her my experience with the Angel Cards. She invited me to draw one more. I diligently shuffled the cards. I noticed my fingers landing on cards, then moving on and finally chose a card. Any guesses? Yep! TRUTH! Five times in a row I drew the TRUTH card. There are, I think, fifty-plus Angel Cards in a set. The chances of this happening are like a gazillion to one, or something huge like that.

I got the message from the Universe, from Aleisha (did I mention there was a crescent moon hovering above the Sangre de Cristo mountains as I drove into Crestone that first night?), and from my soul, loud and clear. Now is the time to listen to MY TRUTH.

Cue the song by Chicago: *"Everybody needs a little time away, I heard her say, from each other."*

The magic that happens in a solitary journey is like a reset of your entire being. This reset is important when embarking on a journey to transform yourself out of pain and into the pleasures of life. It's vital to reorient yourself toward the light of joy so you know which direction to continue moving in. Later I will share a chant with you that uses the four directions and helps to physically reorient you. For now, let's explore something that may have been merely a passing thought or novel idea in your mind.

TIP #6: TAKE A SOJOURN

Time alone is healthy for everyone. Typically it has a grounding effect and allows you to hear the voice of your inherent wisdom. The majority of our days are lived at a full, frantic pace and life does not allow for quiet reflective time that leads you to your truth. Personal sojourn or retreat, *alone*, is extremely renewing and inspiring.

The idea of venturing off by yourself for a week or ten days may be overwhelming and out of the question for you. A great place to start is a long weekend by yourself. It could be that you need regular breaks during your week to really begin to hear the song of truth within your heart. Days, weeks, months, years, I've had them *all* in the form of alone time. I have worked with women who have had their own variations of alone time, and without exception each one of them has returned renewed and refocused and more fully awakened to what is the TRUTH of their heart song.

Whether you're grieving or extremely stressed from a myriad of other life experiences, when you are surrounded by people, even those who love and uplift you, you are influenced by them. The energy of their thoughts and emotions affect you. You feel a responsibility to them based on the constructs of your relationship with them. You and your partner have agreements about the roles you play to maintain your home. With your children, no matter their age, you have agreements and responsibilities about how you are in relationship with them. You have obligations to your co-workers and employers. Your extended family, your friends, and your neighbors all have some level of expectation from you.

Can you "hear" the noise? Do you "feel" the pressure? There is nothing wrong with the demands of these relationships whatsoever! When we are in relationship with someone, we want to show up for them, just as we want/ hope they will show up for us. Being in community with others influences the decisions we make, from the food we eat, to the clothes we wear, to our vehicles and vacations. It gives us a sense of belonging, of being needed... a sense of purpose. Via the feedback we receive from being in relationship, we learn about ourselves and others. It's truly satisfying and beautiful. And sometimes we lose ourselves in the energy, demands, and responsibilities to others. Personal solitude brings us home to ourselves.

I remember a particularly powerful moment I once had while in *savasana* at the end of a yoga class. *Savasana* is the final pose of nearly every yoga class, where the student simply lies down on their mat. THIS is where the magic of renewal occurs. This poignant *savasana* experience for me occurred about the same time that I made my sojourn to Crestone. I was lying there in the softly lit room, with inspirational music playing. Somehow I allowed my mind to completely let go. I mean, for the very briefest of moments I surrendered ALL of my earthly obligations, dreams, intentions, pressures, and mental patterns. The sense of freedom from all gravity, from all responsibility, from all my past patterning was the most blissful abandon I had ever experienced. It lasted a split second, but the memory of it has remained. I remember my first conscious thought was that this must be what it's like to transition to heaven.

The song of truth that's in our hearts calls us to live our truth with free expression. When that song starts to sing, we can initially become bewildered, scatterbrained, and resistant to that inner vibration, especially if it challenges some of our familiar patterns and important relationships. It ignites our deep inner desires, which can sometimes be scary. In addition, when the light of our inner truth dawns, we may realize that we are DONE tolerating some situations, behaviors, and expectations of those close to us. Often we feel that entertaining our truth will lead to a shift in how we are in relationship with our community. We can literally sense the apple cart tipping. Many of us hide or stuff that truth and carry on showing up in the same way for everyone else and denying ourselves.

Denial has a shelf life! One way or another, suppressing your truth will cause a build-up of energy, like water heating in a tea kettle, and eventually that steam will need to release. It can release in an emotional, verbal explosion. It can erupt as a rash on your skin, inflammation in your joints, a racing heart, or a stomach ulcer.

Remember that umbrella of grace I mentioned, the one that appears when you're deep in grief? That grace is an urging from your soul to explore your deepest desires for joy, pleasure and inspiration, as well as both meaning and relationship in your life. Honestly, grief affords us the time and space to explore the deeper panorama and purpose of life.

The most sincere way to allow your heart song to absorb into your conscious mind is in solitude. When you retreat some place by yourself, you gain:

- ▶ Perspective
- ▶ Inspiration
- ▶ Easier breath
- ▶ Better sleep
- ▶ Renewed hope
- ▶ Clarity on your next steps

When you give yourself the gift of solitude, your deepest desires for yourself and for your life can awaken in your mind. In quiet alone time you can hear the song of your soul because it is not being tuned out by the loving, well-meaning chatter and energy of individuals around you.

Again I can hear the "yeah buts" arising. *I don't have the time, I don't have the money, my spouse wouldn't stand for it, my kids would freak out*, etc. Stop the rhetoric. Stop the negative self-talk. Stop the doubt.

One of the biggest questions that comes out of grief of any sort, but especially grieving the loss of a child, is,

"If I'm still here, what am I supposed to do with the rest of *my* life?" You can't truly answer that in the noise, the orchestral song of other people's singing hearts. You must learn to hear *your* song – solo! Learn its tempo, memorize its melody, let it begin to heal you from the inside out. Once you've got it solidly in the forefront of your mind, then you can begin to imagine how your heart song harmonizes with (or without) the heart song of your partner, of your family, of your co-workers, of your community.

This is the foundation of truth for you to take bigger steps toward the truest expression of your joy! And honey, *your* joy is different from your spouse's joy, just as your grief is different from your spouse's grief, because your relationship with your deceased child is different than your spouse's relationship with your deceased child.

There are many, MANY ways for you to experience as much solitude as you need.

▶ You can establish a regular "staycation" day for yourself. Once a week or month.
▶ You can take yourself on an actual retreat, silent or otherwise, but go alone, not with a friend.
▶ You can go to your summer cottage/cabin/beach house.
▶ You can move out!
▶ You can go on a trip.

The possibilities are endless.

Joan Anderson wrote a lovely book titled *A Year by the Sea*. It is an account of her year-long sabbatical from her life. I actually read this book prior to Aleisha passing away and was so inspired by her courage and the insight she gained from her time of solitude. Perhaps in her pages, you will find inspiration or an idea that will be the spark that ignites your own sabbatical, brief or long, to hear the solo melody of your heart song.

YOUR SACRED SOLITUDE

Below you will find questions to help identify which qualities of Sacred Solitude will feel most nurturing for you. While each desire for sojourn is different, I highly recommend establishing an intention for your solitude to have some sort of nature connection. Nature, by its inherent imprint, is soothing, grounding, and renewing. Nature organically reconnects us with ourselves. The purpose of this privacy isn't to be over-stimulated with activities, shopping, or socializing. The intention is to be quiet and listen to your body, your mind, your heart, and your soul. When you listen to these aspects of your being, you are nurturing their expression. Nurturing the truth of your being lays the foundation for reinvention – the idea for what "new normal" looks like emerges.

Questions to help guide you toward a time of solo exploration:

1. Using your Pleasure/Pain Scale, ask yourself what length of time feels most delicious, doable, right.

2. Would you prefer the meditative musings of a road trip? Or the swiftness of air travel? Will you need a vehicle wherever you are going?

3. Consider natural settings like mountains, beach, desert, riverside, etc. What speaks to you of peace, healing, renewal?

4. What time of year are you typically at your best? Most of us

have a favorite season. Fortify your intention by choosing a time of year that speaks to your soul.

5. Consider what natural activity is available that you are willing to engage in while you are there: walking, hiking, surfing, bicycling, yoga, etc.

6. If you don't already have a place in mind, how will you find someplace?

7. Pick three to five words that explain why you need this.

I can almost feel the temptation of some of my dear readers to invite a girlfriend to join you. Resist this temptation! I believe it will serve you better in the long run. Take precautions to make sure you will be safe. Leave contact information with your loved ones, of course. But if at all possible, turn off your cell phone. Leave the TV remote alone. If you must have noise, take along some of your favorite music. If you're afraid you'll go stir crazy with so much silence and solitude, start small. Maybe just a simple overnight at a local hotel. Then allow for your time outs to expand and grow.

Be sure to take your journal along and record any insights, symbols, or messages that come through. For those of you who are curious about Angel Cards, you can make your own or purchase a set on Amazon or through Barnes and Noble. I recommend The Original Angel Cards by Kathy Tyler.

I mentioned in my Crestone story at the beginning of this chapter that there was a crescent moon hanging above the mountains as I drove into town that night. Crescent moons are my personal nature sign from Aleisha. After she left, we noticed waning crescent moons in nearly all her of artwork. The waning crescent moon occurs at the end of the moon's cycle. It represents the crone aspect or the wise woman. It's a time for inner reflection, renewal, and letting go. My family and close friends have a ritual of saying hello to Aleisha during any crescent moon phase, waxing or waning. I often receive texts from people telling me that they saw an Aleisha Moon. It was no coincidence that there was a beautiful crescent moon hanging above the mountains in the midst of the coral sunset that evening as I drove into Crestone on what would become my sojourn toward My Truth!

CHAPTER 7
Quiet Mental Churning

"You've been criticizing yourself for years and it hasn't worked.
Try approving of yourself and see what happens." – Louise Hay

IN CHAPTER THREE, WE TOUCHED on the light as well as the shadow aspects of the mind and how those darker thoughts can cause you to get stuck in the retelling of your story, over and over again. This ongoing storytelling often becomes more dramatic with the telling. That keeps you anchored in pain and disconnected from pleasure. Again, I want to reiterate that I'm not suggesting you stop telling your story altogether. I'm encouraging you to find a more collected way to share it that allows you to stay in neutral energy or better, rather than getting caught in a downward spiral of grief and loss. If you are two or three years out from the initial loss, this is the perfect time to begin the journey to reclaim your joy.

In this chapter, we're going to take a deeper dive into the games the mind plays as a way to protect us. We'll see that while the mind is trying to protect, what really happens is that it enables us to stay stuck in old mental patterns that don't allow us to grow. As we explore these mind games in a fun and humorous way, we'll release some tension and create space to consider the activities of the mind in a more positive, useful light. We want to be aware of our mental patterns and use them to propel us forward on our path to joy.

Connie was a midlife woman who was a participant in one of my group coaching programs a few years ago. She had lost her early teenage son to leukemia three years prior. Her three remaining young adult daughters were the light of her life, however she was on the brink of becoming an empty nester, which was sending her deep into an identity crisis. She was unhappy in her demanding job where she was not appreciated for carrying the company with her high sales volume. Her marriage was strained as she carried the load of being the main breadwinner while her husband struggled to find a new job. She was mired in the mental sludge of grief over the loss of her youngest child as well the pending end of motherhood (in her words) and the extreme stress from the responsibilities of her work and the financial demands of her family.

Connie was aware of her need for extreme self-care and even indulged in a few practices like weekly dinner dates with her husband, regular bath nights with a good book, and girl time with her adult daughters and/or girlfriends. But she was drowning in the sorrow of her loss of her son to leukemia, and the emptiness caused by her youngest daughter going off to college. The loss of her identity as a mother was more than she could bear.

This is an excerpt from Connie's introduction of herself to the group: "I can't take a stand for myself. People will think I'm a bad, selfish person if I do that. I can't leave my job. I know it's affecting my health in a negative way but I have bills to pay. I have to be there for my husband. I have to be his cheerleader. He's so depressed. I can't believe I'm done being a mother. What is left in my life? I'm so tired, but I don't sleep at night. When I come up with ideas of things I'd like to do to for myself, I feel guilty. I should be there for my family."

Connie was stuck in a downward spiral of negative thoughts. Any attempt to show her a more positive perspective was met with a weak, "Yeah I know...." followed by a powerful, "But I can't."

I introduced Connie, and the rest of the group, to the antics of the inner lizard.

INNER LIZARD GAMES

The inner lizard is a delightful concept that is detailed in Martha Beck's book *Steering by Starlight*. With clever humor, Martha describes the inner lizard (or inner critic). The idea is that we all have an imaginary inner lizard inside our mind that has developed from our reptilian brain – the part of our brain that contains the brainstem and the cerebellum. This part of the brain controls our body's vital functions, but also is our instinctual reactor. If we feel an impending attack or doom, it is our reptile brain at work. A mother bear has a similar reactor when she feels her den or cubs are being threatened. In us humans, the reptile brain can get wildly out of control and can take us down a path of lack or attack on a daily basis.

You may hear yourself, or someone you know, repeatedly say things like,

- ▶ I don't have time to take care of myself.
- ▶ There's never enough money.
- ▶ I'll never get a raise at work, they don't even know I'm there.

▶ My kids don't appreciate me.
▶ I'm terrified to drive on the highway.
▶ My family always criticizes my efforts over the holidays. No
   matter what I do it's never good enough.
▶ I'll never meet a nice guy. They're all taken!

This is an example of the inner lizard at work. You know what I'm talking about. We all have one! That inner lizard sits on your shoulder and constantly whispers bitter critique in your ear, creating anxiety, extreme self-doubt, and, often, immobilization. Words often associated with inner lizard messages are, "you never, you always, you should, you shouldn't." The symptoms of what I call Inner Lizard Games are:

▶ They ignite fear
▶ They zap your confidence
▶ You become immobilized
▶ You're tired all the time
▶ They cause forgetfulness
▶ And more!

TIP #7: QUIET YOUR INNER LIZARD

Drawing from Martha's outline, here are my five steps to quiet the frantic games of your inner lizard:

3. **Name Your Lizard**. It sounds so simple, but seriously, giving your lizard a name helps to place him/her sort of outside your consciousness bubble so you can respond with more detachment to its rhetoric. Saying something like, "Oh Sylvie. I know you're worried about driving to work today, but I've

got this. I'm very careful and always watch out for the other drivers," is far less agitating than, "I hate driving to work. It's so scary. I just know someone is going run into me."

4. **Get Familiar with the Lizard Game**. As mentioned above, the name of the game for your inner lizard usually centers around *lack* — there's not enough time, energy, money, love, etc. Or attack — you're going to get hit, someone will mug you, your kids will get hurt. Keep in mind that inner lizards LOVE to blow things out of proportion. They can get very dramatic with fear, worry, and depression.

5. **List Your Inner Lizard's Top 10 Tunes**. I love this suggestion from Martha Beck. We ALL have them. The top 10 tunes are those old familiar messages that play over and over and over in your mind. You may have had some of these since your youth. Write them down in your journal or on a post it note and set a match to them! Burn Baby Burn!

6. **Find the Riddickulus!** Literally find the "riddikulus" (to use a Harry Potter term) in your inner lizard's antics and laugh out loud. There's a great scene in one of the Harry Potter stories where Professor Lupin is trying to help students overcome their fears. "Riddikulus is a charm that is used in defense against a Boggart (something scary). It causes the creature to assume a form that is humorous to the caster," he tells them. In the scene, Ron Weasly sees a larger-than-life spider approaching him. Upon Ron casting the Riddikulus spell, the spider appears with roller skates on all eight legs and stumbles and falls and doesn't reach him. You can do the same with your inner lizard's messages. Your inner lizard latches onto fear. Shift the energy of those fears by finding the ridiculous-ness in them. Make them as funny as you can to loosen the grip of fear those messages have on you.

7. **Placate Your Lizard.** — With power! Martha suggests that

you mollify your lizard with a treat, like a grape or a cookie or a piece of chocolate — always a good idea in my opinion. Whatever it takes to zip it! Then powerfully (and audibly if necessary) tell your lizard, "Sylvie (insert YOUR lizard name), I've got this covered! Go lie down and take a nap. You're not needed here." Remain in your power as you take a step forward on the path toward joy... and notice that as you step out, while your lizard's voice may be raging, his/her volume will dissipate quickly with your bravery and successful forward progress.

I realize this is quite light and silly, but it's powerful. My students frequently comment on the antics of their inner lizards. They love how this simple, five-step process helps them acknowledge the patterns of their mind. By animating and personifying this part of their mind, many of my clients avoid beating themselves up.

"Caring kindly for the reptile, rather than either believing it or struggling against it, is the way out of dread and into peace."
— Martha Beck

THE MIND CONFUSES AND IMMOBILIZES

When your inner lizard is on the loose, in other words your mind is racing with negative thoughts, this has the power to confuse and immobilize you.

One of my clients, Susan, is in her mid-fifties. She lives in the suburb of a large city. She is out of shape and needs to get moving to become healthier. She is terrified to leave her house. Her inner lizard has convinced her that she will be attacked by a stray dog or even another human, although she lives in a perfectly safe neighborhood. She is a brilliant woman who loves being in nature and walking. She is confused between her desire for health and well-being and the fears of her inner lizard. This confusion immobilizes her, causing her to rationalize staying inside her home day after day and sitting in front of the television.

When you're in the hollows of grief, inertia is so much easier to bear than the perceived energy required to get up and get happy again. You inner lizard has a heyday when you're stuck in grief, because you're vulnerable, exhausted, and confused. Like Susan, you may be in a safe and supported environment to blossom into joy, but your inner lizard fears have immobilized you. Add to that any fear and/or guilt you may have as you falsely believe you will forget your heavenly child. "I can't stop grieving. The sorrow keeps me connected to my son or daughter. If I become happy I will forget them. I can't live with forgetting them."

We will address the idea of forgetting your heavenly child in just a minute. First, let's take a look at how the mind can invalidate the emotions.

THE MIND INVALIDATES TRUE EMOTIONS

One of the mind's major sabotaging antics is to make us believe our feelings are wrong. In our society, we put more value on the mind than the emotions, and we are quick to discredit any intense feelings. Making the emotions wrong helps to keep you immobilized and rooted to your disbelief that you can be happy again. Ignoring the feelings forces the body to store that emotional energy, usually as discomfort, pain, or tightness. This physical tension becomes so prominent that it distracts you from experiencing pleasure. Feeling pain is familiar and we tend to gravitate toward what is familiar even if it's not in our best interest. Grief sort of gives us an excuse to remain the victim of these unfortunate circumstances. Can you start to see the vicious cycle that we keep ourselves in? That is, until someone comes along and has the guts to tell you to pick yourself up, dust yourself, turn yourself around and start over. You Can Do It!

I've stated before that the body stores those intense emotions that our inner lizard refuses expression of. The large joints and muscles of hips store much unexpressed emotional energy as tightness, radiating to low-back pain. When the knees ache that's a clear sign to ask yourself, "What do I 'kneed?'" This is listening to the body. The messages of the body will invariably return us to the unexpressed emotions of the heart.

THE MIND MAKES THE EMOTIONS WRONG

Your inner lizard is rather terrified of your emotions. That's because from a young age we were taught not to trust our emotions. Here's an overly simplified example: Maybe you had a beloved toy as a child and it got broken or lost. Imagine the devastation to your young child heart. You may have cried, thrown a tantrum, or sulked – and your parents quite possibly told you, "Don't be sad. We told you not to lose your toy." Instead of having your sadness and loss honored, you were shamed and told to ignore the truth of your heart experience. Your heart was likely screaming, "Wait! But I AM sad. So I'm wrong for feeling sad that my favorite toy is lost?" Do you see how your true feelings were invalidated? Your parents weren't trying to be malicious. But there is definitely a disconnect between how you are being told to feel and how you truly feel. Our impressionable child minds learn to discredit the emotions and make them wrong.

When it comes to dealing with the emotions from the standpoint of the rational thinking mind, it's important to get the mind to align with the emotions so they can work together. There is one simple step that has the ability to magnetize the mind and emotions. Truly it is SO simple it can seem trite. But it isn't. Are you ready?

Listen to your emotions. What are your feelings saying? Even if their messages seem childish, irrational, or out of control, listen to them. If you ignore them or brush them off, you are ignoring the truth of your experience in any life circumstance. This is how you became disconnected from pleasure. You quit giving credence to your feelings. The energy of those emotional experiences are still there inside you. Your body, in its great wisdom, is going to hold on to that ignored, unexpressed energy until you're ready to deal with or release it. Imagine all the years and years of stored emotional energy you have! It's time to get the mind and emotions in alignment and start releasing this pent-up tension.

You may be asking, "What is the balance between listening to and feeling the emotions and not getting sucked into a downward spiral of self-pity?" In my own journey and in witnessing the path of many coaching clients, I have observed the mystical calm that descends when the emotions are heard and considered and sometimes expressed in a healthy manner. If the inner lizard is at rest, the rational skill of the mind steps in and names the feeling. For instance, "I feel overwhelmed with sorrow. I

feel invisible. I feel heavy with sadness. I feel pulsing rage."
The mind, by naming the feeling, validates the experience
of the heart. The magical benefit of this is that it affords
you the ability to observe your heart experience clearly,
which allows you to process the feeling and move beyond
it with greater ease. Truly, it requires discernment and
practice to bring the feelings of the heart and the thought
patterns of the mind into alignment for the highest good of
your entire being!

More than anything, your emotions want to be heard.
The mind (imagine your inner lizard here) is afraid of
the emotions because they are often *so* strong. When the
emotions are heard and/or witnessed, they sort of settle
down and become easier to deal with. If the mind resists
giving attention to the emotions by ignoring them, that
e-motion (energy in motion) becomes more agitated.

THE MIND – KEEPER OF MEMORIES

Perhaps the sweetest benefit of an active mind is
its ability to remember. Our memories comfort us and
allow us to experience the pleasure (or pain) of a past
moment as often as we want. This recall ability is one
of the most positive aspects of the mind. Remembering
can have a delicious, pleasurable, and aligning effect on
your being. The negative potential, of course, is to get
stuck in the past.

Remembering is an important part of healing. We can
feel proud, satisfied, and even hopeful with the re-minding
quality of memories. At the same, time we can listen to and
honor the emotions of sadness, extreme disappointment,
despair. Sitting in this circle of polar opposites with an open

mind is a powerful healing experience. Imagine your heavy sadness and despair holding hands with your pride and hope as you remember. Breathe deep into this awareness and know that all aspects of your being – body, mind, emotions, spirit – are benefitting as they realign for your highest good and your potential for living a purposeful life.

There are many ways to activate memories of your child's life. You probably have traditions that you engage in regularly to keep those memories alive. Obviously looking at family videos, photos, and cherished personal articles are all ways to ignite a memory or two. Revisit the power of the senses from Chapter One. The power of scent and sound, in bringing up memories, is astounding. One of my favorite memory prompts comes from other people. I absolutely love it when one of Aleisha's friends posts a picture on Facebook that I've never seen before. Or I love to hear them tell a story about her that I've never heard before. This awakens a new energy, a new awareness of her that I didn't have previously. Invariably it ignites my own memories of her. This is a very pleasurable, exciting experience for me.

Take some time today to observe how your lizard is at play with negative mind games. Discern how to pacify him/her. Then shift your awareness to the pleasurable ways your mind helps you remember and heal. As I mentioned earlier, grief is consuming and disorienting. By not resisting it, but working with it, we can learn to turn ourselves around and get back on track to reclaiming joy.

We're changed now, not because she/he left us but because she/he touched us.
– Greeting Card Sentiment

CHAPTER 8

Use Sound to Soothe

Peace. It does not mean to be in a place where there is no noise, trouble or hard work. It means to be in the midst of those things and still be calm in your heart.
— Author Unknown

IN THE LAST CHAPTER, WE witnessed the antics of the lizard brain. That pesky reptilian brain can really work us into a physical, mental, and emotional tizzy! But how can we quickly and effectively quiet the out-of-control spin of the mind until we have the time and space to do our inner lizard work?

In this chapter, you will learn techniques that you can use in a moment or two to soothe the anxiety that arises from the inner lizard freak-out! Grief, and his partner in crime, Worry, have a tendency to take control of the mind. They settle in, establish roots, and then multiply and grow. They love to play the same songs of fear, sadness, and depression over and over again. This repetitive rhetoric can easily take you on a long, dark detour away from joy, keeping you stuck in sorrow. Taming the racing thoughts of the mind and finding stillness for answers to arrive are both key steps along the journey to joy.

In her most fairy-esque way, Aleisha was a whimsical, wise sage... at the age of 17. She had the unique ability to witness her teenage worries, frustrations, and her feelings in general with an incredible measure of humor and self-compassion. She could articulate what she was feeling and where it was coming from with clarity, most of the time. In high school, she had a French teacher from whom she just couldn't seem to pull an A grade. This was particularly frustrating for my Type A daughter who easily pulled As from English, math and science. Aleisha was passionate about French. She fell in love with the language and had dreams of doing a semester abroad in college. So she was quite motivated to learn as much as she could. Frequently she would come home from school and vent her frustrations about this teacher.

I listened as she shared her side of the story of not being able to please this woman enough to garner an A grade, even though she was completing assignments as directed, on time and to the "nth" degree – as was Aleisha's modus operandi. Sometimes she would talk loud and vehemently. Sometimes she would even tear up in overwhelming frustration. And then, without my nudging, she would inevitably giggle, take a deep breath, and say, "Calm yourself!"

This became a bit of mantra that she would use on herself and others – me, her dad, her brother, and, I suspect, even friends. She always stated it with love, lightness, and humor. There was usually a twinkle in her eye to match her ever-present smile.

Calm yourself. These simple two words carry some potent energy, especially when considered with a deep, stress-relieving sigh.

We are fortunate in this day and age to have so many classes, workshops, books, and teachers of calming techniques. You can access hundreds of these free online resources with a simple Google search. I'd like to share a few of my favorites that are quite simple and have served me, at a moment's notice, over many years.

TIP #8: USE SOUND VIBRATION TO CALM YOURSELF

Sound therapy is gaining scientific and cultural popularity. Also called vibroacoustic therapy, it involves using tones, music, and chanting to bring a harmonic, calm, and healing state to a person. I know school teachers who are using music to elicit calm yet potent learning environments for their students. I know of hospitals who are using music therapy to aid in the healing and/or harmonic deathing of patients. We all have experienced the uplifting nature of fast-paced music – alpha waves – and the soothing nature of slow-tempo music – beta waves.

When I owned a yoga studio, there were days when I was driving to the studio so exhausted that I had no idea how I was going to teach another class. I had a couple of songs cued on the playlist in my car that I would listen to repeatedly to give me a mental and physical energy boost so I could teach my class. On the flip side, more often than not, I play relaxing music in my yoga classes nowadays. Most of my students arrive on their mat from a highly stressful day at work, holding tension from long, congested commutes and clinging tightness from family distress and other life issues. They don't need any more mental stimulation. What they need is a softer, more beta experience to guide them to peace at the end of a workday. They need to reconnect to the peace that always resides within their heart. As they bend and stretch and twist and move, they release tension, their faces relax, and their general demeanor is more radiant and calm.

Om is a chant, a sound vibration traditionally associated with yoga. It's such a simple, primordial sound. It really has no meaning and yet contains all knowledge. Shortly after I completed my yoga teacher training I took a Sanskrit for Yogis workshop offered by the lovely Katyayani Poole. I already knew that Om, when broken down, contained three distinct sounds. Katyayani explained the vibrational significance of each of these sounds a bit further. The following is my interpretation of what I learned from Katyayani.

A (aaaaaaah) – resonates in the belly, the third chakra – your place of personal power and self-esteem. Say it now. Take a deep inhale and just allow a strong, resonant Ahhhhh vibrate out of your mouth. See if you can "feel" a vibration in your belly.

U (uuuuuu) – resonates in the heart, the fourth chakra – your container for love, healing, dreams, and desires. Inhale deeply and release a long slow Uuuuuuu sound. Can you sense a vibration in your heart center?

(It's important to note that for the purposes of this book, the heart chakra is connected of course with our physical heart and the lungs – both of which are deeply impacted by grief... and resilient with joy.)

M (mmmm) – vibrates in the head, the sixth chakra – your mind, the vessel of insights, intuition and visions. After a complete exhale, take a deep inhale and let go of an extended Mmmmm sound. This one easily produces a vibration in your head.

Mmmm is my personal favorite. It's the one I use most often, especially at night when my mind is racing. It's also quite useful just prior to meditating as it helps to quiet those racing thoughts, to some degree, that tend to distract from a satisfying meditation practice.

Now, just for the fun of it, combine all three sounds in one long exhale. See if you can make each sound last about the same amount of time. AhhhhUuuuuMmmmm.

The simple practice of Om-ing is a tool you have available at any time, day or night, to calm yourself. It's quite easy to do this quietly, in the midst of a class or meeting, when someone else is speaking (or yelling!). You can bring resonant alignment in the midst of an argument, while in traffic, or during an emotional breakdown of your child (or spouse). As mentioned above, I use this frequently to calm my racing thoughts at night when I can't get to sleep. It's simple and easily adaptable to most life circumstances. You can use the complete Om sound or just its parts.

YOGA POSES TO CALM THE MIND

There are as many opinions about which yoga poses are best for stilling the mind as there are yoga teachers. What I present here are some simple favorites of mine, based on my own experience and the observations of my students. It's important to practice these movements slowly along with slow, conscious breathing.

Yes, No, Maybe So – Seated on the floor or in a chair
Simple, SLOW yes nods (three times), followed by no nods (three times), followed by maybe so nods (three times) can bring a realignment of the vestibular system while at the same time resetting mental energies to a more neutral place. Naturally you can pause at any

point in the sequence to hold the pose to bring greater relief to tense muscles. Just be sure to breathe as you are holding the pose.

1. Come to seated alignment with your feet on the floor, your shoulders in line with your hips, and your ears lined up over your shoulders, chin parallel with the floor. This is neutral.

2. Exhale all your air out and on your inhale, lift your chin up slightly. Be careful not to collapse in the neck completely by tilting the head all the way back. You can pause here to slowly open and close your mouth to bring some relief to the jaw for extra benefit. On your next exhale, slowly release your chin to your chest and feel the lengthening occur in the back of your neck. Repeat three times.

3. Starting at neutral with eyes gazing forward, take a deep inhale and on your exhale gently, slowly turn your head to the right. Inhale as you come back to center and exhale turn your head to the left. Repeat slowly three times. Don't go to the point of strain or pain. We're just trying to release tension in the neck and calm the mind with this particular practice.

4. Finally, again beginning in a neutral seated position with your chin parallel to the floor, take an inhale and on your exhale gently, slowly release the right ear toward the right shoulder (keep the shoulder still). With the inhale lift your head back to neutral and on your next exhale release left ear toward left shoulder (keep the shoulder still). Repeat three times. When you're complete with this series, do several rounds of shoulder rolls forward and back.

Child's Pose

Word of Caution: Only perform this pose if you are able to get up from the floor by yourself and if you have no trouble with your knees. You might want a block, a blanket, or a pillow for this one.

1. Begin on your hands and knees. Make sure your toes touch and your knees are apart. Keeping your arms extended, bring your buttocks to rest on your heels. Continue to extend your arms as you lower your torso toward the floor, eventually bringing your forehead to rest on the floor. You can stack your hands or use a yoga block or pillow to support your forehead. Your arms can stretch overhead or wrap around your knees if you aren't resting your forehead on your hands. Keep your breath flowing naturally. With your forehead resting on the floor or your block, gently, slowly rotate your head side to side. Imagine that the thoughts in your mind are softening and dissipating as you hold this pose and breathe.

2. This is a pose that encourages us to return to innocence. As you release your thoughts imagine settling into a more pure state of being. Hold the pose for the space of five to ten breaths, according to your comfort level. To leave the pose, bring your hands underneath your shoulders. Push up yourself up using your hands while simultaneously lifting with your core muscles.

Legs Up the Wall (or Chair)

1. This is one of my personal favorites for deep relaxation, especially before bed. Simply lie down on the floor. Try to get your buttocks as close to the wall as possible. You may want

a blanket or pillow for your head or under your buttocks, depending on the flexibility of your neck and hamstrings. Lift your legs up the wall, allowing the wall to support them. Legs can be bent or straight. If this causes too much strain in the hamstrings, scoot away from the wall a bit to allow greater comfort. This pose is typically very comfortable and deeply relaxing for most people. A variation, especially for tight hamstrings, is to lie down on the floor and lift the legs, then rest them on a chair, sofa, or ottoman.

MEDITATION TO CALM YOURSELF

Meditation is a bit of a "hot topic." I'm sure you've heard of the many benefits of meditating. And you might also have experienced the frustration of a wandering mind, a common affliction when embarking on a meditation practice. I'm not going to get too deep into meditation here. There are many effective resources to guide you. In my opinion, the best, most effective way to experience success at meditating is to experience it firsthand. Start by checking your local community recreation center. Many local rec centers are now offering both yoga and meditation classes. A Google search on meditation books, CDs, or DVDs will give you an endless variety of teachers and techniques to explore. There is a lovely app for your cell phone called Insight Timer. You can set your own chime to begin and end your meditation. You can see how many people around the world are meditating with you. And they even have some pre-recorded guided meditations. Guided meditation is the best place to start. Also, I have found that using soft music in the early days of meditating gives the brain something to focus on while you get used to the meditative state.

A word about walking meditations. I once had a meditation teacher tell me that walking meditation is not meditation. I beg to differ. Being outside, listening to the natural sounds around me, even hearing the rhythmic fall of my foot on the walking path, lulls my mind into a soothing meditative state. Notice that I don't mention the use of music. Music while walking can be beneficial, but you miss the nurturing quality of the breeze through the trees, the buzzing of bees, the birdsong, the chirping of prairie dogs, etc. If your mind is particularly busy, though, listening to soft music while walking can bring you to a more meditative experience.

I recorded a short, guided meditation just for you. It's a variation on one of my most requested guided meditations.

I have used this meditation personally, in yoga classes and retreats, and have found it to be transformative for both me and my students. I hope you enjoy it. You can find it at www.griefinterruptedbook.com.

CHAPTER 9

Explore the Art of Chanting

"Often it is the deepest pain which empowers you to grow into your highest self."
— Author Unknown

I ATTENDED A RETREAT SEVERAL years ago where the guest presenter was a Celtic master teacher named RJ Stewart. He taught us some of the basics of Celtic tradition, including the energy and workings of Merlin and the faerie realm. I was especially interested in his teachings on the faerie realm, as Aleisha had an affinity for and a collection of fairies, since passed on to me. But the most impactful thing I took away from that retreat was RJ Stewart's Crossroads Chant. A description and meaning of this chant can be found in his book *The Spiritual Dimensions of Music* (www.rjstewart.net). The best way to experience this chant (and other elemental chants) is to order his CD *Elemental Chants*, available at the website above.

I have mentioned the disorienting nature of grief several times. When I carry out this chant, I always feel like I have reoriented myself in the time and space of this planet on which I live my life. I feel like my mind and my heart are in alignment. I am calm, clear-headed, and ready for the day. Because this chant invokes the energies of the four directions, coupled with the energies of the elements, it seems to provide a powerful centering experience almost without exception.

TIP #9: PRACTICE CHANTING TO REORIENT YOURSELF

Drawing on the energies of the four directions and four elements, here is a brief description of my interpretation and meaning from practicing this chant over the course of several years. Obviously these descriptions are based on awareness from the Northern Hemisphere perspective.

East – Air energy: symbolizing the mind, new beginnings, the dawn of a new day, fresh ideas

South – Fire energy: symbolizing spirit, action, motivation and confidence

North – Earth energy: symbolizing the body, grounding, stability, ancient wisdom

West – Water energy: symbolizing the emotions, ending and completions, letting go

To perform the chant you simply use the vowel sounds in this order:

The sound of the East is "Eeeeee."

The sound of the South is "Iiiiii."

The sound of the North is "Aaaaaah."

The sound of West is "Ohhhhhh."

We draw energy from Divine Source and Gaia into our heart center through the sound of "Uuuuuuu."

All sounds are the same monotone with the exception of "Uuuuuuu," which carries a high note, a low note, and a return to the middle monotone note.

I believe that anyone who has experienced profound stress or trauma can find it especially healing to reorient themselves with the world in which we live. When we are aligned energetically with our physical environment, there is a much greater ease to everything we do. There arises a spacious potentiality for joy to germinate.

NEW NORMAL

Returning to the source is stillness, which is the way of nature. The way of nature is unchanging. Knowing constancy is insight.— Lao Tzu

Establishing a new normal after a devastating loss means reorienting yourself by uniting the wisdom of the mind with the energy of the emotions. Nature automatically neutralizes and calms us to be able to bring about this alignment. Soothing beta wave music can have a similar effect. RJ Stewart's Crossroads Chant is another very effective tool in establishing a new, resonant vibration of normal within you. It is from here that you can begin taking real action toward change.

You see, it's important to address the more tangible aspects of physical tension and shallow breath first because those are easily accessible. Next we want to calm the rhetoric of the lizard mind with nature and sound vibrations. This paves the way for deep emotional healing. We must practice these simple techniques to allow space for the heart to express and return to its expansive, loving nature. This path of healing is true no matter what the trauma is.

By allowing the emotions to have space to BE, we create an internal environment of safety and awareness. Our emotions are able to express what our minds would never allow because of the antics of the inner lizard and the rampant expectations of cultural "shoulds and shouldn'ts." You see, to some degree the mind wants to conform, to fit in, to be connected to a tribe. Belonging in our community gives us a sense of being needed and connected. And yet we all have experienced a time when that tribal culture isn't always an exact fit. The emotions rise up to express what the mind resists. But the mind has veto power, so to speak, and often makes the emotions wrong in order to dictate behavior. It's a crazy, freaking political battle within.

YOUR EMOTIONS ARE NOT WRONG!

Let me say that again:

Whatever you are feeling, in any given moment, is not wrong. The outward expression of those emotions is when we often get in trouble, by using harsh words and engaging inappropriate actions.

The disconnect between the heart and the mind creates a dissonant vibration within your being. Chanting and sound vibration brings an alignment between your thoughts and feelings.

Valerie came from a hardworking, middle class Midwestern family. Hard work was a way of life. She raised four kids with her husband while working full time in a food processing plant. I met her in my yoga class when she was at midlife. She appeared to be well-adjusted and had a healthy sense of conservative humor. In one particular class, the theme was around releasing stored emotional energy and specifically allowing that release through tears. Valerie spoke up and said, "I haven't cried for years! I do tear up at commercials now and then but my mind just won't allow an all-out cry. I actually wish I could." Upon further exploration, I learned that Valerie's mind would immediately negate any emotional expression of sadness. She would convince herself that these feelings were silly and unreliable and she just needed to snap out of it. Interestingly, Valerie had had both a hip replacement and a knee replacement by the time I met her. Her heart longed to weep to express those long pent-up emotions. But her mind wouldn't allow it. I noticed that with focused breath work Valerie experienced some relief. Chanting seemed to make her uncomfortable until I mentioned that hymns are a form of chanting and suggested she listen to Gregorian chants. I left this issue alone with her. After about two months, Valerie came to class with a huge smile on her face and her blue eyes twinkling. She told me how much joy and relief she was experiencing singing old hymns to herself.

Your emotions are simply energy – E-motion – energy in motion. They only have a positive or negative charge because of what your mind thinks about them... or how your mind "judges" them according to codes of our culture. Consider this – we categorize the primary emotions like this:

Love and joy = Good

Fear, anger, sadness = Bad

But really, all of those emotions are just energy vibrations. They have a frequency (high/low), a pattern, perhaps even pressure. I like to refer to the emotions as a barometer reading for what's truly going on internally.

The word *barometer* is defined as an instrument measuring atmospheric pressure; anything that shows change or impending change. It comes from the Greek word *baros*, meaning weight.

Imagine the weight of your emotions while in the throes of grief. Then consider the pressure of the emotion of happiness. Can you feel the difference in their weight? You might notice a heaviness in your heart or your gut when you are in the depths of sorrow. When you feel joyful, it's likely you feel quite light on your feet.

Imagine running an errand at the grocery store. There you are having a rare respite from the heaviness of grief. You're pushing your cart through the store and all of a sudden "that song" comes on – and you can't escape it. You can't shut off your ears or turn down the volume. Before you know it, you're standing in the dairy section with tears streaming down your face. Children ask their mommies what's wrong with that lady. Men freak out and walk in a big arc around you. Other women look at you with pity. You were fine and then you weren't. Just about the time you collect yourself you bump into someone you know who "expects" you to be heavy with sadness. You can literally FEEL the barometer reading of your emotions indicating a crisis and/or a change.

I want you know that it is okay for you to feel light, happy, loving. You don't have to pretend otherwise for anyone. And, it is okay for you to feel overcome with sadness. Remember the umbrella of grace? That grace allows you to ride the winds of constant emotional change. No expectation or explanation required.

After the "year of firsts," the extreme barometric swings

of emotions begin to level out to some degree. What I hope for you is that you will be tender, loving, and careful with your heart as you start to feel pleasure again and reclaim your joy. Feeling pleasure and reclaiming your joy first requires that you pacify your inner lizard so that your heart feels safe. This creates a safe, nurturing environment for the heart to express its true delight and happiness. When the mind makes the emotions wrong, the expressions of the heart get stifled and they don't get processed. That unexpressed energy gets stored in the body as tension, pain, and dis-ease.

"How are you doing *today*?"

This is typically how I check in with those who are in grief. I'll pose a check-in question with as much emotional neutrality as possible because I truly don't know how someone who is grieving is doing from moment to moment, day to day.

I remember having days when I was actually feeling neutral – around 0-1 on the PP Scale. I'd be out running errands and run into someone I knew and they would hug me, tear up, and ask in a very pitying tone, " How aaarrrrre youuuu?" I always felt like they expected me to dissolve into a puddle of tears. What they didn't know is that maybe I was emerging from the puddle and had just finished drying myself off, fortifying myself with a good pep talk so that I could navigate public life without falling apart. THAT can be a huge milestone, right?

The path to reclaiming your joy requires that you listen to and honor all of your emotions. It implores you to be gracious with yourself and use your mental acuity to align your thoughts WITH your emotions rather than against them. When you become proficient at this TLC of the heart, you will propel yourself forward by leaps and bounds.

Do not be afraid of bad news. Keep your heart steadfast, trusting in the Lord.
Keep your heart secure. Have no fear. Look upon your foes in triumph.
— Psalms 112:7,8

(We found this verse taped to Aleisha's computer after she passed away.)

CHAPTER 10

Name Your Feelings

Desire is at the root of our divine impulse to evolve. Desire leads the way home.
— Danielle La Porte

MANY YEARS AGO, I LEARNED to scuba dive. Understand that my entire life I have had a simultaneous fear of and curiosity about water in general and the oceans in particular. I truly desire ocean energy on a regular basis and have an equally strong desire to interact with/observe aquatic life. When I learned to scuba dive, I took all of my classroom and initial water training in Colorado at a local recreation center. But to be able to participate in open water dives, I had to do an open water certification. My husband and I did that certification on a quiet beach on Maui.

The instructor was very kind, patient, and encouraging. I donned all of my scuba gear and started to follow my instructor and my husband by walking out into the ocean from the beach. As the water became deeper, rising up to my chest and chin, the softly rolling current kept splashing in my face. I panicked! I started breathing shallowly, my heart was racing, and my mind was saying, "Mayday! Mayday! Get back to the beach! You can't do this! You're going to drown!" (Can you picture my inner lizard on my shoulder freaking out?).

The men could see the panic in my eyes and they both kept encouraging me to put my face in the water. My inner lizard went ballistic with this news: "Are you freaking kidding me?" it shouted as I frantically shook my head back and forth telling the boys, "No! I can't!" They persisted with their crazy insistence that I put my face in the water and all would be calm. Somehow, someway, I reached beyond the insanity of my mind and briefly remembered my desire to see the coral, the fish, the beauty of the ocean and... plop! I did the unthinkable and put my face in the water. Then, without thinking, I leapt off my feet and submerged my entire body in the water. And guess what?

It was so incredibly peaceful. So amazingly calm. And the beauty was all that I hoped it would be and more! I actually started giggling through my regulator. I could feel the soft waves of the ocean current moving above me. But underneath them was pure oceanic bliss.

My mind threatened to eliminate my desired feeling to connect with the ocean because my inner lizard was freaking out about a perceived impedance to my ability to breathe – yes, even WITH the regulator in my mouth. In this chapter we're going to look at the relationship between the desire for a joyful life and the feeling state that having that life will bring, and how the mind might try to sabotage you.

TIP #10: NAME YOUR FEELINGS

In the last chapter, I briefly mentioned the relief and alignment that occurs when the mind simply gives a name or identity to the feelings (expressions of the heart). Again, this is such a simple practice that it's easily overlooked. Let's explore this a bit more, together.

Consider your current feeling state. How do you feel right now? Identify your emotions with feeling words: I feel safe, agitated, free, loved, happy, worried, etc. Before we move into how you desire to feel, take a moment and describe how you *don't* want to feel. Maybe you feel worried about something right now. In addition to not wanting to feel worry anymore, you might also not want to feel fear (worry's twin). Knowing that you don't want the experience of fear creates an environment for you to identify that you want to feel peaceful and confident. You have just established the feeling state you desire to move into.

In the last chapter, we took a look at how the emotions are like a barometer reading for what is truly going in your mind. E-motions are emotional energy expressed as feelings, or stored in the body if expressing them isn't available.

In her powerful work *The Desire Map*, Danielle La Porte takes you through a process of identifying your feelings and listening to them in an intimate way. Early in the process, Danielle says, "Feelings are how you perceive life. Perception informs how you live." This is in alignment with the notion of feelings being the barometer reading that tells you what's truly going on inside you and influences the choices you make.

Giving attention to the emotions rather than ignoring them is vital to the healing process and reclaiming joy. However, the mind has a tendency to sabotage those efforts. It's easy to get the thoughts and the emotions mixed up. The mind likes to take over and do just that. This often results in invalidating the experience of the heart. In spite of the mind's tendency to take over, the mind and heart truly work in concert with one another, influencing each other. They do a sort of back and forth dance.

Experts and masters in New Thought, Mindfulness Training and the Law of Attraction encourage us to understand how the mind affects the outcome of our lives. For instance, if you constantly observe your bank account from the perception that there isn't enough and you repeatedly speak to that notion, you will regularly attract life circumstances that validate that thought. You will always live in a state of scarcity. In that regard, what you think becomes reality. When you constantly observe your body as fat, ugly, or unhealthy, you will keep yourself in exactly the state that you don't desire, instead of the experience you DO desire.

When you decide to reclaim your joy, you've got to acknowledge the grief that is always there. Just love it, in its tender vulnerability. Next, take a moment to identify that you don't want to get stuck in the victim mindset or any other debilitating emotion that comes to mind. Finally, name and own how you want joy to show up in your life. What additional emotions would help you experience as much joy as possible in your current state? Keep in mind that your capacity for experiencing joy will expand as you practice claiming your joy moment to moment.

DISTINGUISHING BETWEEN THOUGHTS AND FEELINGS

What are the feelings behind the thoughts? Perhaps you've had an argument with your partner. Let's say he criticized a big project you're working on. He vehemently cried out, "You're wasting your time on this. Just watch a

YouTube video and be done with it." If you inquire gently of your partner, you might discover that he is *feeling* quite worried about the toll your big project is taking on your health and well-being, as well as the impact it is having on your relationship.

If we were to look beyond the feelings, we would find a deeper desire within your partner. Perhaps his desire is to feel connected with you. His rational mind may be telling him that desiring connection is weak and unmanly in the light of your demanding project. This could make him feel threatened, insecure, and concerned, which would lead to an outburst. His thoughts are literally invalidating the more potent message from his heart. This disconnect exacerbates the situation because of the confusion between his heart and his mind. Interestingly, I have observed this very situation occur numerous times between couples who are grieving the loss of a child. There are so many overwhelming emotions, and the rational mind is trying to make sense of it all. The emotions typically get stuffed, which causes the pressure to build and eventually leads to painful outbursts.

The heart feels what it feels. It often experiences a longing, a calling, an unexplainable urge to express a certain way. When we allow the heart grace-ful space, the energy of those feelings begins to evolve into conscious thought which will spur you to action – and/or change.

Let's tell a story, perhaps YOUR story:

You were catapulted into the storm-tossed sea of grief when your child passed away. You've navigated the deep, dark waters of the "year of firsts," and here you are two, three, five, eight years later, perhaps still tethered to your little dinghy of grief and being tossed to and fro in the raging storm sea of sorrow. From time to time, you see a golden light on the horizon. You may have a hunch what that warm glow represents, but you aren't entirely certain and are absolutely not confident you will ever arrive to experience that warm glow of light. The golden light represents your new normal. Its name is Hope. But sitting here in your dinghy of grief, you don't even truly realize that it's hope. You simply feel a pull toward this light because it's warm and you're oh-so-cold and wet from grief. You have a strong desire to move toward the light and feel warm.

At this point, your inner lizard may be freaking out and saying things like, "You don't have the energy to get there! There is only one paddle. So how are you going to move toward the light? You don't deserve the light. The light is too far away. It will never happen. You can't have hope and certainly not happiness. You're supposed to be grieving for crying out loud!"

That's just your mind trying not to "create waves" – but ironically, that's exactly what it's doing. Your mind is afraid of your feelings because it thinks that if you go deep and look at those strong feelings, you'll lose control. In fact, the opposite is true. When you go a little deeper and identify your feelings, you will find a clarity that will lead to calmness. Naming your feelings allows the full spectrum of emotions to live side by side in you. And truly, sorrow and joy can hold hands in your happy, purposeful life.

Right here, right now, write down any feeling state you have. Use feeling words, as opposed to thinking words. I'll help you get started:

I feel peaceful, agitated, restricted, free, inhibited, lonely, invisible, sad, glad, clear, confused, foggy, neutral, ugly, beautiful, healthy, depressed, inspired, worthy, abundant, grateful, angry, and so on.

There many, many feeling words. Use thesaurus.com to help expand your verbal repertoire. Spend some time getting intimately familiar with how you are feeling now. Especially notice any feelings that seem to be ongoing or chronic – positive or negative.

I'll say it again: please write them down. When you *write* about what's going on internally, you – well, you get it out! – Literally! And when you get your feelings (and your thoughts!) OUT, then you can look at them more objectively, which allows you to discern how to reorganize them or gain a new perspective on how to deal with them.

I'm assuming that since you're reading this book you have some level of desire for a new way of living that is sustainable as well as pleasurable. We're calling that Reclaiming Your Joy! So here you are, with your desire for joy fresh in your mind. Using your vivid, active imagination, begin a list of feeling words that describe in even greater detail what your new life of joy and meaning could look like. This becomes how you WANT to feel – in other words, your desired feelings or outcome. Be sure to make pleasure, play, and whimsy a very real part of that "new normal" experience of life.

For the last several months or years, you have unconsciously allowed the overwhelming feelings around your grief to dictate your daily life. That was the norm for that time. Now, I'm inviting you to wake up and reclaim your desire for a joyful life. The timing is different for everyone, but I believe that once you've passed the "year of firsts," you can slowly (or quickly) begin the courageous journey of taking your life back.

Aleisha's message to me shortly after the accident was just that. "Wake Up, Mom! Be who you REALLY are! Stop hiding!" Aleisha was encouraging me to awaken to the Truth (there it is again!) of my desire for my life. Who do I truly want to be? How do I really want to show up in the world? What impact do I truly wish to make? This has been a significant part of my journey to joy in the years since Aleisha transitioned to heaven.

I want to ignite that desire to wake up, in you. It takes great courage to rise up out of the hollows of grief and claim your life with purpose and joy. It is far, far more admirable to dedicate your life to being happy and making a difference, in honor of your child, than it is to wallow in the quicksand of self-pity and sorrow that will shackle you to the victim mentality and depression for the rest of your life. Wake up, dear friend! The mountaintop experience of joy is waiting for you!

LOSING CONTROL

Before we move on to soul agreements, I want to mention the confusion that can arise when we fear our strong feelings will race out of control.

It is quite common to shy away from exploring the feelings. It makes us feel vulnerable. And feeling vulnerable evokes feelings of helplessness, powerlessness, loss of control....sort of like that moment when you got the news that your child had slipped the bonds of earth. We never want to experience that again, and therefore it's tempting to overlook this step of getting specific about our current feelings and our desired feelings. You may find that you do need to indulge in an emotional breakdown. That's actually a good thing, as it's an energy release. Tears, sobbing, screaming, stomping your feet, shaking your fists, or slugging your bed pillow are outlets for that pent-up emotional energy.

This release creates space, which then allows you to look at the feelings in detail and name them. Naming your feelings will bring a clarity and calm that passes understanding. When you identify your feelings, the chances of an out-of-control spiral are far less, because your heart has been heard. Your mind is happy because it knows what it's dealing with and can categorize that energy in a way that makes mental sense. This prevents an inner lizard freak-out. Your emotional heart is calm because you have listened. The body doesn't have to store excess, unprocessed energy in motion. Simply naming your feelings is a powerful healing tool that brings you to a neutral place where you can more effortlessly move toward joy.

This walk of grief will always be a part of your life. As with any trauma, you will process it in layers. With each layer you will receive greater relief and move closer to the mountaintop experience of joy.

CHAPTER 11
Consider Soul Agreements

Remain established in your calm center and everything will take care of itself in ways far more miraculous than you could ever manipulate. –Alan Cohen

MY SPIRITUAL MENTOR ONCE TOLD me that God put a very special part of Himself/Herself in each one of us. The particle of God that is in you, only YOU have. No one else has it. God chose you to come to this planet and express this aspect of Himself/Herself because the planet needed that particular spark of energy at this time. Your soul is "the keeper" of this God energy, this spark of the Divine. In addition, your soul holds the intention for your life purpose. The pulse of this vibratory intention radiates from your soul into your physical, mental, and emotional being. You utilize this energy through your physical, mental, and emotional expressions. Most of us live the intention of our soul unconsciously. My goal is to increase your awareness of your soul to empower you to live with renewed purpose and joy.

This chapter and the next could be a challenge for you. That's OK. I will share my thoughts. I'll suggest books that really spoke to me. And then I'm going to encourage you to explore the concept of your soul in depth and according to your belief system. We don't have to agree here. But I do invite you to read these pages with an open mind.

WHAT IS THE SOUL?

I often refer to the soul in my yoga class themes. I usually have only a minute or two to present a concept that is vast and somewhat unexplainable. I find that simplicity allows for the easiest integration into the mind that is already overcrowded with information. My intention isn't to preach, but rather to illuminate a concept that allows my students to develop their own awareness and relationship with their soul. So I try to share my thoughts in a clear and concise manner.

My simple mind conceives the soul as this: The soul is the eternal part of your being. It is that part of you that is always connected to Divine Source: Human + BE-ing.

WHY TALK ABOUT THE SOUL

In my opinion, it's important to talk about the soul when we are dealing with death and grief. In Western culture, death is considered a failure. We are always seeking to preserve our youth, abhorring the aging process. In the medical field, one of the most respected industries on the planet, aspiring physicians are trained to save lives and prevent death. When a patient dies, many physicians will say something like, "We lost the battle."

In the days, weeks, and years since Aleisha's accident, I have come to believe, without a doubt, that death is not a failure! I believe each soul has a contract for a fairly accurate (though not exact) number of days in this life. And when they exit this planet – no matter what form that takes! – it is because their mission in life was complete. I believe that Aleisha's mission was complete and she was able to leave this planet. My mission is not complete – yet!

Talking about the soul of a person (of ourselves even) helps our feeble minds and aching hearts to grasp that our loved ones are fine! They are alive and active in the soul realm, doing their soul stuff, watching over us and, yes, trying to communicate their love and encouragement to us in a variety of ways. Talking about the soul brings a continuity instead of finality to our connection with them. It infers a continuation of existence as opposed to an end.

Considering the nature of the soul and the purpose of the soul can elicit peace and help us make sense of what has happened. Soul awareness assists us in organizing our thoughts, emotions, and physical sensations so we can heal, and allows us to pull the scattered pieces of our heart back together so that joy can begin its beat within our being.

With our perceived broken pieces coming together, when thoughts are arranged in a way that makes a modicum of sense, with joy building a presence, we start to feel whole again. Within that wholeness a new, normal way of living emerges, and we can find meaning and purpose in life again.

HEEDING THE CALL OF OUR SOULS

For as long as I can remember, I've been a spiritual seeker. My seeking has taken me into the teachings and the structure of major religious beliefs and beyond. I've been questioning dogma for years in order to better understand why I'm here and what I'm supposed to do. Asking deep questions is definitely one of the byproducts of the path of grief. Some of my biggest questions have been, "What am I supposed to do with my life now? If Aleisha's mission was complete in seventeen years and mine, in my mid-fifties, isn't yet, then what is my soul up to? What does my soul wish for me to accomplish still?"

Perhaps I'm working out karma with my husband and son and/or nurturing relationships with other family members and closest friends. My daily life experience has me continuously pondering the deeper dynamics of relationships in general, so I know that being a lifelong observer of all relationships plays some role in my soul's purpose for this life. I love meeting new people and hearing stories from their lives. I also feel a strong pulse from my soul to be M.A.G.I.C. – Making A Gigantic Impact in the Community. All of these concepts are my soul speaking to me, guiding me, and helping me stay on course with my soul's intention for this life.

What exactly does "make a gigantic impact" mean? That is a delightful mystery that I get to step into every single day. I'll share more about M.A.G.I.C. at the end of the book. For now, I hope the partial description of my soul's intentions is providing a more expanded awareness and curiosity of your soul and its intentions.

Your soul is speaking to you. Your call is different than mine. I believe the request is strong for you to heed this divine petition. You're still here. You can still make a difference in this world. Your mission, should you chose to accept it, is to say Yes to your soul purpose, to that God particle within you.

SOUL AGREEMENTS

When Aleisha passed away, it was utterly inexplicable. Truly she was vibrant, giggly, and alive one day, one moment, and then she was gone! How could that be? Police officers questioned us about her mental state, inferring that she was suicidal. HA! Not Aleisha! She was excited to live, to go to college, to grow up and begin her career. So how did we make sense of it?

When I made the comment, at the beginning of the book, that "At some point you agreed to this," did you bristle? I did, when my friend first said it to me and my husband just a few days after Aleisha passed away. That is the LAST thing we wanted to hear, because it suggested that we planned this tragic loss. That we agreed to it, that we said YES to it ... which, of course, we don't recall because we had been living unaware of our soul's intention and oblivious to the agreements we've made with the other souls with whom we are incarnating.

I will tell you that now, more than twelve years later, this comment brings me comfort. But it's been a long road to get to this point. The reason I can say that it brings me comfort is because of what I now believe about my soul, Aleisha's soul, and our soul agreements or contracts.

WHAT ARE SOUL AGREEMENTS?

Two books that were instrumental in bringing me to an understanding and peace about soul agreements are *Journey of Souls* and *Destiny of Souls,* both by Dr. Michael Newton. Dr. Newton is a counselor for behavioral disorders and a Certified Master Hypnotherapist. Despite having a skeptical nature, he stumbled into conversations with numerous souls, via hypnotherapy. These souls were willing to share with him what happens when a loved one dies. In *Destiny of Souls*, Dr. Newton states, "It is our souls that make us human on earth, but without our bodies we are no longer [human beings]. The soul has such majesty that it is beyond description. I tend to think of souls as intelligent life forms of energy."

Before I get too far into the nature of souls and soul agreements, I want to make a statement similar to one Dr. Newton makes:

Understanding the soul was an important part of *my* healing journey toward a new normal. The more I read, the more I wanted to learn. There are a lot of well-meaning individuals wanting to do good work in the world but who are not experts. I am not an expert! I explored many different sources and found that Dr. Newton's work spoke directly to the questions I had. Nothing I read conflicted with my personal belief system. I encourage you to have an open mind and *to use your personal power and mental acuity* to research what feels right for you. This is YOUR Journey to Joy and your library of supporting resources may not be the same as mine.

From the book *Destiny of Souls*, I learned that our souls have a life on the other side. There is structure and order and learning. There are groups of souls who gather together for mutual growth experiences. These "soul pods" serve as wise counsels to one another. They observe their fellow "soul mates" as they incarnate on the physical realm. There is knowingness and communication between souls within the pods regardless of physical incarnation or heavenly presence. Generally, individual souls agree to incarnate together to help each other have experiences of learning and to impact life on the planet through awareness. There are also souls from other pods who agree to show up to provide peripheral support and contribution, though not necessarily as impactful as the original group of souls. You can observe this to be true in your life when you consider the various people in your life. Your parents. Your siblings. Your spouse(s). Your children. Your best friends. These relationships were likely agreed upon before you incarnated. Taking into account free will (each individual's right to choose) these relationships have developed according to a plan that is flexible according to those individual choices. You can also see that you are in relationship with people on different levels, some rather peripherally. ALL relationships are opportunities to learn about yourself and how you *relate* to others.

Soul agreements, whether vital or peripheral, are always, always mutually beneficial. Both souls, in relationship, are served in the learning process. Even in situations that we judge abusive, horrific, or immoral, there is significant learning that takes place on a soul level. Does this mean that these acts of immorality are OK? Does it mean they are approved by beings on the other side? No. Often, though not always, there is some karmic realigning taking place.

A word about karma: karma is often written off as penance for some bad behavior in a previous life. While that can be true, it's not the totality of what karma is about. Sometimes a soul will agree to show up to play "the victim role" to help "the perpetrator soul" gain insight and/or amend a previous life trauma – and vice versa. In addition, there are souls who take up the call to bring awareness to atrocities and or dis-ease in this world. Often these are atrocities and dis-eases that are asking for greater awareness in world in order to initiate reform and healing.

TIP#11: CONTEMPLATE YOUR SOUL AGREEMENTS

Think about all of the people who have entered and exited your life. Have you learned from these relationships? THAT is the real purpose behind all relationships. To grow, to learn about ourselves, to learn about others, and likely to help others learn about themselves.

The last twelve years have shown me that saying YES to life is much more fulfilling and infinitely more pleasurable than staying intimately connected to my grief. This has led me to a new normal life that is far more joy-filled than I could have imagined twelve years ago. I'm still learning to listen to my soul in those still, quiet moments. And I still try to thwart its intentions. I'm quite adept at exercising my free will and resisting my soul's messages. But my soul's intention for my life is much, MUCH stronger than my earthbound opposition. My soul is patiently persistent and sends messages to me repeatedly until I acquiesce. When I finally surrender, I'm ALWAYS so glad I did. I know that I know that I know that my soul truly has my *best* interest at heart.

I want YOU to have the wisdom, the awareness, the certainty that the Divine light that is your life, with all of your joy and sorrow, is still needed on the planet. Your soul has a mission that will help you serve the planet AND help heal you day by day, year after year.

Do you feel it? Do you hear it? That call from your soul? Does it scare you or confuse you? Can you consider the notion of soul agreements between you and significant people in your life? Would your journey and these concepts be easier to process with someone to talk to? If you answered yes to any of these questions take another step toward conscious alignment with your soul. Do some gentle yoga to release physical resistance and clear your mind with my short chair yoga class. Explore meditation by listening to my guided meditative journey. Visit www.griefinterruptedbook.com to partake of these gifts or send me an email to ignite further discussion at info@coreystiles.com

Your life of joy awaits you!

CHAPTER 12
Review Your Life Now

When you do things from your soul, a river moves through you.
Freshness and a deep joy are the signs. –Rumi

IN THE LAST CHAPTER, I introduced you to the writing of Dr. Michael Newton and his discovery of souls and soul agreements. Dr. Newton, with the aid of his clients, shares explicit detail about the personality of souls, the "age" and experience of different souls, what happens upon death and birth, the counsel souls receive and about a soul's "life review."

LIFE REVIEW VS. JUDGMENT

Life review was of particular interest to me as it gave me some insight into what we all might experience when we leave this planet. And it was in reading life review stories that my understanding of soul agreements, or contracts, expanded.

Some belief systems teach that when we die we experience a judgment at the hand of God. Many, many followers are terrified of this final judgment. Take a moment and consider the idea of a life review rather than a life judgment. Doesn't this feel much more benevolent and merciful? Consider the scenario of a newly transitioned soul. Imagine that they are *reviewing* how they lived the life just departed. In this life review, they are sitting alongside their guardian angel, their spirit guides, and previously departed loved ones discussing, pondering, inquiring of circumstances, choices, and the outcome of the life. If we take into account the statement my spiritual mentor offered, "God puts an aspect of himself/herself in each of us," why would God *judge* Himself/Herself in me, in my life? Judgment feels like it is based more in a closed, controlling mindset, rather than in expansive celestial wisdom. I like to imagine, when anyone passes away, that they are sitting in a lovely space with their soul pod and guides discussing/debriefing what went on in their life. I can imagine that wise council asking the soul, "How did you feel about that event and your response to it? What did you learn from it? Are you complete with that issue or do you need to learn some more?"

TIP #12: REVIEW YOUR LIFE NOW

I now have a regular practice of reviewing the events in my life. I try to adopt a higher spiritual perspective. Because I review often, and make amends when necessary, I have few regrets in life. Having little or no regrets is a building block for living a life of joy. I believe that we all can take inventory of where we're at and how we're doing now, before we leave the planet. It makes us much more conscious about how we are living day to day and we still have time to make course corrections along the way. Things to consider in a present-day life review are:

▶ How are you taking care of your God Pod — the vehicle you get to live your life in?

▶ What mental patterns are you hanging onto that keep you miserable, stuck, unproductive?

▶ Are you listening to your emotions and using them to guide you to a truer, more powerful life experience?

▶ Does your life have meaning and purpose to YOU? Do you feel there is anything else that you are being called to do?

You may have noticed that this book addresses four aspects of your being: body, mind, emotions, and soul. My intention is to help you build a greater awareness of what's going on in these areas of your being, especially in the wake of extended grief, in order to help you start to reconnect with pleasure and joy and live a meaningful life according to your soul's purpose. By becoming mindful of the body and valuing how it stores energy, you can consciously release excess energy stored as tension and choose more pleasurable experiences through the five senses. When you become aware of the positive and negative aspects of the mind, you can re-pattern your thinking to serve your life intention better. As you listen to your emotions and consider their message of truth, you can begin to discern your reactions to people and life circumstances. Awareness of all of these qualities will serve to align you with your soul. To ascertain these deeper concepts requires stillness. Connecting with nature puts you in a still, neutral state to find that clarity. Prayer and meditation also give you pause to allow soul messages to come into your consciousness. It is here, in the still quiet moments, that God/Source/Spirit, *through your soul*, can "speak" to you about your life.

I saw the following years ago. It's a gentle reminder that our souls and God are over "there" watching, waiting patiently for us to listen, to surrender, to say YES! Yes to our mission. Yes to the plan that we agreed to.

Be Still and Know that I Am God

Be Still and Know that I Am

Be Still and Know

Be Still

Be

It should be noted that your soul "speaking to" you isn't always auditory. Sometimes the message is visual. Sometimes it is cognizant. Maybe you'll feel a sensation on your skin. And then there are the signs and symbols and synchronicities.

TRUST THE SIGNS, SYMBOLS, AND SYNCHRONICITIES

Remember my story about the Angel Cards and picking TRUTH five times in a row? I believe that was a sign from my soul and from Aleisha to listen to my truth. To make choices for my life according to *my* truth and no one else's. This "sign" was validated for me by the symbol of the crescent moon hanging above the mountains in the evening sky as I drove to Crestone. Since that time, I have a regular practice of merging my rational mind with the barometer of my feeling state to make decisions that are often guided and validated by signs, symbols, and synchronicities. I refer to these with delight as magical moments. Once you start paying attention, you will find that they are everywhere!

Magical moments pop up in my life regularly. So many have occurred in the process of writing this book that my mind is swirling with magical energy! Because I love magical moments so much, I should be used to their presence in my life. But I'm still delighted and surprised every time a seeming coincidence shows up. These synchronicities are always moments of pleasure for me that are like bank deposits in my joy account.

You see, everything is energy. Every plant, animal, rock, human being, house, car, food, water... it's all energy. Energy doesn't die. We humans are conscious energy in a human body. Our souls are also conscious energy, not in a human body. The point here is, our departed loved ones are conscious. They can communicate with us. And YOU can communicate with your loved ones on the other side. You can admit any mistakes and ask for and receive forgiveness from them, which allows you space to forgive yourself. You must forgive yourself! And then you are set free. Free to get about creating a life of joy.

When you embrace the idea that our loved ones are energy and that energy doesn't die, then you can begin to accept the signs and symbols they use to communicate with us. You see, our soul friends and loved ones are vibrating at a level that is much higher than the vibratory energy here on Earth. In order to communicate with us in a way that we can grasp, they have to slow their energy way down. It's much easier for them to use signs, symbols, and synchronicities to communicate with us. And here's a secret: you don't need a medium to do the communicating for you. You have the ability to communicate with your loved ones just as you are.

The following are just a few ways our heavenly soul friends communicate with us:

▶ Blinking lights – electricity is easy and accessible for them.
▶ Nature symbols – nature is neutral. It doesn't judge. So it can receive imprints that are meaningful to us in order to get a message across.

▶ An alignment of events in our favor. It's not that they are
up there pulling puppet strings. But they do have ways of
arranging circumstances that lead us humans to exercise
our free will and bring an alignment to life circumstances,
aka magical moments!

▶ A song, a statement by someone you know or a perfect
stranger, a book title. These are all ways that our loved
ones communicate with us.

▶ Rocks shaped as hearts on the sidewalk during your
walk, crosses in the sky, fairy statues in unusual places,
or whatever symbols are meaningful to you. When these
show up unexpectedly, it's okay to believe it's a sign. In all
likelihood, it is.

I distinctly remember Aleisha coming to me while I was
lying in *savasana* one evening in my yoga class. First I felt
her vibratory presence quite strongly. Then I "saw" her in
my mind's eye. The vision was not crystal clear. It was a little
blurred around the edges. She kept trying to "come into me."
I kept saying, "Oh, no, sweetie. It's OK. You don't have to
come back. I'm OK. I'm hurting and sad, but I'm OK." Later
I was relating this story to my spiritual mentor. He said, "Oh!
She was trying to hug you." Ha! That is SO like Aleisha!

Allowing the possibility that signs, symbols, and synchronicities are really attempts by your son or daughter to
communicate with you helps you feel so much better. And when
you feel better, when you feel happy, when you experience more
pleasure, you automatically reclaim some of your inherent
joy. When you resist this possibility you stay stuck in grief.
In addition, the simple act of *allowing* this communication
prevents you from forgetting about your departed child.

Start a list of the signs, symbols, and synchronicities
that your transitioned loved one left, perhaps before they

passed, or keep a list of ones that have held potent meaning for you since their death day. Write down their meaning to you. These symbolic messages are one of the benefits of being under that umbrella of grace.

Remember my friend Paula? Since her son, Luke, passed away several years ago, she has engaged in a whimsical relationship with him based on numerous signs. Paula notices more crosses in the sky and has more heart shapes show up in her coffee cup, on the walking path, or on a restaurant receipt than she ever noticed prior to Luke's transition. She captures these magical moments inevitably with a laugh, a "Hi Luke!" and her cell phone camera. She has established a new relationship with Luke.

As I processed my grief and pondered, "What am I supposed to do NOW?" I also came to realize that I needed to learn to have a new relationship with Aleisha. This new relationship has evolved over the last twelve years, much as our relationship would have evolved were she still here. It's taken a different and unexpected turn, but I'm starting to remember the agreement we made before coming here. And I can tell you we're right on track. I have no regrets.

A WORD ABOUT REGRETS

Many people live with the weight of regrets. This heavy emotional energy can be as debilitating as grief. Living free from regrets does not mean that you don't make mistakes. We all do!

I've had several people ask me if I have any regrets. I can say with all honesty that I have very few. Does this mean I've lived a perfect life? Ha! No way! I'm human just like you. I didn't always make the right choice in parenting my kids. I'm certainly not a perfect wife, friend, daughter, sister, business owner. I mess up all the time. Often I know when I have screwed up. And there are times when I'm completely clueless. Two key actions have allowed me to be imperfect and live without regrets:

- ▶ I admit to myself and to the other person that I've made a mistake.
- ▶ I say, "I'm sorry."

There is SO MUCH freedom in these two simple steps. Almost always, these two steps nullify any residual negative energy from a wrongdoing and open the way for healing for all parties.

Do yourself a huge favor. Set yourself free from regrets. If you are carrying regrets associated with your deceased child, then sit quietly and have a conversation with the soul of your child (or any departed loved one). Examine the situation. Own your mistake. Then say, "I'm sorry." Those two words are among the most powerful words in our language. They bring immediate relief to both parties involved, whether those parties are living on Earth or in heaven.

I know many people who really struggle to get those two words out. While that is an entirely different subject for an entirely different book, I strongly encourage you to make these words a regular part of your vocabulary for the remaining days of your life. This is living from wholeness and with more acute mindfulness. You can literally review your actions, your life circumstances, on a regular basis and relieve pressure that has the potential to build up and either explode or cause you to remain stuck in sorrow, self-pity, and depression.

In Conclusion

You are in the room to heal the room
You are in the space to heal the space
There is no other reason for you being here.
— A Course in Miracles

I LOVE THIS QUOTE BECAUSE it re-minds us that each one of us is here on the planet for a reason. No matter how light or dark a person's life is, there is a point to it. And that point, inevitably, is to bring awareness, to heal the planet in some way. It is easy to become discouraged, depressed, and to feel hopeless at the many atrocities taking place on this big blue marble. If we allow it, we can become enmeshed in darkness and our countenance turns cynical. Even if cynicism is your path of choice, there is purpose in that. Sometimes the darkness of the cynic is exactly the perspective that's needed to reveal the counterpoint of astounding light. Conversely, there are times when light is so strong, so powerful that it burns. I can hear your "yeah buts" here: "Too much light? Is that even possible?"

There are two kinds of light – the glow that illuminates and the glare that obscures.
– James Thurber

People say to me over and over, "I don't know how you

125

do it." The thing is, I don't have a choice. THIS is my life. And this is yours if you are in the throes of grief. Where we have a choice is in how we show up to meet what our soul contract intends. We have to have faith that there is a purpose to the soul agreements we established before we came here. We have to re-member (realign) that energy, knowing it will all be okay in the end.

The memories of our time with Aleisha and the legacy of her vivacious energy fuel Kevin, Grant, and me. Her vibrant energy, her love for us, live on. We feel them every day. I believe the four of us agreed to "do life" together. I also believe that part of that agreement was for one of us to leave early and help/support those left behind from the other side. Part of our mission is to cultivate a deep love, a profound gratitude, and a resounding respect for each other, for all of life on the planet and for ourselves. Inherent in that mission is M.A.G.I.C – Making A Gigantic Impact in the Community.

Having an inkling of what my soul is up to in this life has brought me significant peace. This spiritual peace has propelled me forward on the path of not just mentally reclaiming my joy, but living my joy. Within this blue bubble of peace, I was able to extract a reason for everything in my life, from the traumas to the exhilarations. Perhaps more than anything, knowing that all is well on the soul level helps me to move through uncomfortable life circumstances with greater ease. This has led to an overall contentment with my life. Any challenges or frustrations are temporary, albeit uncomfortable. The place where I have the most control is in how I think about these situations. I still get fired up about some things. My inner lizard is alive and well, playing her Top 10 Tunes regularly. My life isn't perfect, but it IS wonderful. More often than not these days, I'll text my husband the following message, "I Love My Life!"

How did I get to this place of peace, certainty, and contentment? I experienced my daughter passing out of this life and into the heavenly realm. I listened to what others were saying about her, how she was remembered. I searched and searched and searched for an explanation of the afterlife that spoke to the truth I felt in my heart. I imagined my beautiful, happy, vibrant, loving, friendly daughter doing her life review with her wise celestial council and I asked again and again, "What am I supposed to do NOW?"

After going through my year of firsts, grieving all that was lost when Aleisha transitioned from this realm to the next, I began a journey of deeper self-reflection and life review. I had to get clear about what my soul is up to for the remainder of this life. That journey of practicing all the incredibly simple techniques I've shared with you here, led me to today. I am happier than I ever thought I'd be again. I am grateful beyond measure. I see beauty in the world and its people. I am curious about people's stories. I have an expansive respect for everyone, even those whom I don't agree with. And I LOVE.

My soul contract with Aleisha? We agreed to come into this life as mother and daughter. I felt that powerful soul connection the minute she was born. Her soul's plan was for a short, but potent mission. She accepted it and accomplished it and she left a positive imprint in the world. To this day, people tell me of how their lives have been changed because of her. And the ongoing expression of our soul contract is for us to work together, from both sides, to cultivate more joy, more laughter, more hope and healing in the world. In short, our soul agreement is to be M.A.G. I. C.!

When a tragedy happens, like the death of a beautiful child, we naturally find ourselves pondering the meaning of life. Grief gives us 20/20 perspective on the impact and purpose of our beloved's life. When we eulogize the departed, we coronate them in a way. We dignify their life with the remembering and review. The memories lead us to identifying a point to our son's or daughter's life that to us seems unfairly shortened. When we can see the point, we can at some level – perhaps subconsciously – make some sense of this unexplainable loss.

Grief is now your life companion. But it doesn't have to be a dominant figure. Grief will add a depth of color to your life of joy. It will bless you with a more poignant perspective on even the insignificant events of life. Grief awakens you to the pain in others and invites you to reach out with an encouraging hand of hope. Grief encourages you to observe and live according to the truth of feeling in your heart. And though grief is heavy and all-consuming, it becomes a launch pad for you to rise up into a life of joy and service, in memory of your most precious child.

When you uplift another with help and hope, you heal yourself.

You don't have to take up the mantle of joy and service. Unless you do. If your soul is calling to you to Wake Up, Rise Up, Look Up, chances are there is something in the mission statement for your life that will keep calling until you answer. And if you don't heed the call?

You do have free will. You can say no to joy and service and yes to sorrow and stagnancy. What will the result of that be?

Profound spiritual depression and a life of utter misery.

Your spirit needs movement. It needs to flow, to express. Depression is when the energy of our soul (our spirit) stops flowing. It sort of backs up on itself and becomes a toxic cesspool of e-motion.

Dear one, please join me in heeding the call to M.A.G.I.C. – Making A Gigantic Impact in the Community. We agreed to this experience of grief to help raise awareness, to help heal the planet in our own unique way. Grief's invitation to us is to take the pain and transform it in to joy.

Your uniqueness is God shining through your soul. It is an aspect of God that the world needs right now and that only you can bring. By embracing life, by reaching out and grabbing as much life force as you can, you let the light of your soul touch others and the blessing is mutual. When you choose a life of joy, you are not only investing in the remaining days of your life, but you're also ensuring that your impact in the world will be positive and your life review will be rewarding.

I've shared with you tools that helped move me out of the hollows of grief and into a life of joy. This transformation didn't take place overnight. The tools were effective because I was dedicated to putting them into practice. The more I practiced, the better I felt. The better I felt, the more I desired a new normal filled with as much joy as I could contain. Just like the downward spiral of depression, there is a corresponding upward spiral of inspiration when you choose a life of joy. The word inspiration means to be "in spirited."

The following quote is from my friend Sarah Entrup, who is a spiritual life coach. It has become my personal motto:

Creation is what happens through me when I'm connected to my wholeness and inspired by my life.

May you find a new trajectory to your life, inspired by all the events that have led you to this point. Join me on the journey to joy, and honor the legacy of your transitioned loved one.

Additional Reading

Steering by Starlight, Martha Beck
Living from the Heart, Puran and Susanna Bair
The Original Angel Cards, Kathy Tyler
A Year by the Sea, Joan Anderson
The Spiritual Dimensions of Music, RJ Stewart
The Journey of Souls, Michael Newton
Destiny of Souls, Michael Newton
The Desire Map, Danielle La Porte

Acknowledgements

THIS BOOK MOST CERTAINLY WAS not a solo venture. There was influence and encouragement from numerous sources on this Big Blue Marble, as well as from the heavenly cosmos.

Firstly, my dear Aleisha, being your mom is one of my greatest pleasures and accomplishments in this life. Your shining example of joy, fun, and respect continue to guide me and keep me on track. Our agreement is continually re-membering itself to me. I'm beginning to recall the plan for this life and how we would work together from both sides. I'm awake and I'm ready for the next phase. I love you from the depths of my soul, my sweet girl.

I've had many teachers, coaches, and author mentors who have helped guide me to my inner truth, which allowed me to sculpt my own path of growth and purpose. Dr. Leland Kaiser, my unofficial spiritual mentor: thank you for bestowing upon me and others your deep wisdom on the wings of love and grace. Kevin Kaiser: for showing up and holding incredible spiritual space for our family – all four of us – as we navigated this transition and for sharing insights that became the new space for us to step into, my deepest gratitude for you, dear friend. Sarah Entrup: thank you for being a cosmic cheerleader and for sharing a quote with me that has become my life mantra. Sandi Faviell Amorim: thank you for being my cosmic twin and for your bubbly yet gentle encouragement. My author friends, who I'm quite sure are my Cosmic BFFs – even though we've not met yet! – Neale Donald Walsch, Alan Cohen, Martha Beck, Elizabeth Gilbert, Danielle LaPorte: your influence took me on the deepest soul search and lead to the re-cognition of the light within.

Angela Lauria, your program is brilliant! Your ability to hold space for so many authors to make a difference in the world is extraordinary. Thank you for your ability to hold the vision, carry the belief when we authors lose it temporarily, and for cheering us on endlessly. I bow in deep gratitude to you. Namaste.

Maggie McReynolds, I'm pretty sure we are soul sisters. Your loving and humorous editing kept me on track and true to the needs and feelings of my ideal reader. Thank you for being YOU! What a perfect match you were for me. I can't wait for our two mimosa dates!

To the Morgan James Publishing team: Special thanks to David Hancock, CEO & Founder for believing in me and my message. To my Author Relations Manager, Megan Malone, thanks for making the process seamless and easy. Many more thanks to everyone else, but especially Jim Howard, Bethany Marshall, and Nickcole Watkins.

From the other side: Grandma Jean, your love and sense of humor are part of my everyday life experience. Oh, how they help in tense times. Erminea, Elkanar, Tnarg, and Shelayah, what a ride this life has been. Let's do it again! We're a GREAT team! Eldon, you're keeping this vehicle in good shape. Thank you!

To my family and community, you may have been on the sidelines observing, but I felt your enthusiastic support all along the way. Your belief in me is humbling, and I thank you from the bottom of my heart. Tina, my SSF, there were many days that you kept me going with your unique humor. Thank you! Paula, who woulda thunk the similar paths our lives have taken? Love you girl! Lee, the blue bubble of peace reigns supreme – and so do carnitas! Shirley, your love and support mean the world to me. Will, I will ALWAYS love you. You are a gift from her. Mom and Cheryl, in all of the years, all of the circumstances, the aparts and the togethers, I KNOW! Do you?

Grant, to say that I'm SO proud of you simply does not convey the depth of love, awe, and gratitude I have for you. You are an inspiration to me and to many others. What an honor and a privilege to be your mom.

Finally, Kevin, you are the BEST friend, husband, father, and life partner for this girl! Nothing I have accomplished would have been possible without your patience, your support, your LOVE, and your humor. Thank you for making me laugh every day. Always and Forever – No Matter What!!

I Love You All to the Aleisha Moon and Back!

About the Author

FROM THE TIME SHE WAS three years old, Corey's highest aspiration was to be a mom. She would try to dream of other careers, but her dreams always brought her back to motherhood. That dream came true, twice! Motherhood is her greatest accomplishment. The dream was shattered at the peak of her career when her daughter Aleisha was killed in a car accident at the age of seventeen. Devastated, disoriented, and stopped in her tracks as she navigated the "year of firsts," Corey knew, in the back of her mind, that a new normal, a new focus for her life was necessary. But where to start? Drawing from her years as a life coach and her lifelong seeker's heart, she stepped onto her yoga mat. And with each breath, with every gentle movement, she slowly found her inner illuminated path to joy.

Now, more than twelve years later, she has helped dozens of women fuel the flame of their inner light and embark on their own journey to joy. She brings lessons from almost twenty years of life coaching, insights from her years of yoga practice, a variety of spiritual expressions, and a deep love of nature to her writing, her coaching, and her yoga teaching. She has an immense desire to infuse life with that HaPpY, playful energy that Aleisha embodied. She has been affectionately referred to as "Master Encourager" by her coaching clients. People around the globe often reach out to her saying, "I need my Corey-fix."

She is a graduate of Coach U, Martha Beck Life Coach Training, and Cook Street Professional Cooking Program, and is an E-RYT Yoga instructor with over 2500 hours of teaching. She is grateful to live in Colorado, where she enjoys walking her canine kids, hiking, SUPing, and has been known to blow off work to go play in her kitchen.

Thank You

Dear Reader,

Thank you for taking the time to read my book. My deepest wish is that you now have hope that you can live your remaining days with more joy than sorrow, more pleasure than pain, more laughter than tears. It IS possible. I know this because I did it, and so have others. There will be challenges and setbacks along the way. There will still be some stormy days ahead. It takes great courage and tremendous strength to desire to rise up out of the hollows of grief and reclaim your joy and your life. Because you read this book, I'm offering you a free toolkit of practices to use at moment's notice. Of course, the tools in this kit only work if you use them.

RECLAIM YOUR JOY TOOLKIT

12 Tips for Reclaiming Your Joy

1. **Cultivate more pleasure** using the Pleasure & Pain Scale
2. **Let nature soften you,** neutralize you, and begin to heal you
3. **Reframe your storytelling** and let go of the victim identity
4. **Use gentle yoga** to relieve tension in the body

5. **Breathe to Relieve** and bring about renewal

6. **Take a sojourn** for clarity and peace

7. **Quiet your inner lizard** to stop the mental rhetoric

8. **Use sound vibration** to calm yourself

9. **Practice chanting** to reorient yourself

10. **Name your feelings** in the present moment and those you desire to feel in the future

11. **Contemplate your soul agreements** to bring meaning and purpose to your life

12. **Review your life now** and make course corrections along the way

Enjoy this toolkit in one sweet little cyber package. Please visit www.griefinterruptedbook.com to grab your gift. Or send me an email at info@coreystiles.com

I'd love to hear from you.

Namaste

Morgan James
Speakers Group

We connect Morgan James published authors with live and online events and audiences who will benefit from their expertise.